BEYOND THE MOTHER COUNTRY

EDWARD PILKINGTON

BEYOND THE MOTHER COUNTRY

WEST INDIANS AND THE NOTTING HILL WHITE RIOTS

I.B.TAURIS & Co Ltd
Publishers
London

Published in 1988 by
I.B. Tauris & Co Ltd
3 Henrietta Street
Covent Garden
London WC2E 8PW

British Library Cataloguing in Publication Data

Pilkington, Edward
    Beyond the mother country: West Indians and the
    Notting Hill white riots.
    1. Black persons. Attitudes of. Great
    Britain, history
    I. Title
    305.8'96'041

ISBN 1–85043–113–2

Printed and bound in Great Britain by
Redwood Burn Limited, Trowbridge, Wiltshire

CONTENTS

To Jessica, my parents and Baron

'In the history books they tell us the English race has spread itself all over the damn world: gone and settled everywhere, and that's one of the great, splendid English things. No one invited us, and we didn't ask anyone's permission, I suppose. Yet when a few hundred thousand come and settle among our fifty millions, we just can't take it.'

Colin MacInnes, *Absolute Beginners*

Preface

'Riot' is an emotive term. In Britain it conjures up images of incidents which, by virtue of their violence, have become etched into the public memory: Brixton in 1981, Heysel Stadium and Broadwater Farm in 1985. The word has become associated with gangs of football hooligans running amok, or of black and white youths fighting running battles with the police.

On the other hand, rioting by whites against blacks is generally considered alien to British culture and experience. This type of violence is most immediately associated with lynch mobs in the American South. Yet they have occurred in Britain, on more than one occasion. Indeed, the most recent white riots of this sort erupted just thirty years ago, in 1958, in Notting Hill and Nottingham.

The writer Colin MacInnes was so shocked by these incidents that he predicted that, along with Suez, they would be remembered as the key events of the post-war era. They would put an end, he thought, to Britain's claim to any moral leadership in the world just as Suez would dispel any lingering doubts about the decline of Britain's political dominance.[1]

MacInnes was wrong, for despite their undoubted significance, the riots have been forgotten. Apart from those individuals who actually witnessed the violence, most people have only the vaguest recollection and the younger generation is almost entirely unaware that the 1958 race riots ever happened. In the academic world, too, the 1958 riots have been largely overlooked, as the paucity of literature on them shows. This forgetfulness is partly a quirk of history, which apportions undue weight to some events while skimming over others. But that is not the only reason; to some extent the riots have also been intentionally ignored. They were consciously played down at the time, in the hope of minimising the damage caused to the reputation of Britain abroad, and to the Macmillan Government's popularity at home. A member of the House of Lords hinted as much two months after the riots when he said: 'At that time the country received a severe mental and moral shock, and, as with all shocks of that kind, when we got a glimpse of unpleasant feelings just below the surface, we tried to forget. Feelings of guilt and shame are the best possible agencies for ensuring forgetfulness.'[2] Nor was it just the Government that tried to silence discussion of the riots. Even among liberal circles people turned away, as though from a repugnant smell. Three months after the riots a South African journalist who had witnessed them wrote: 'People didn't want to read about the riots; they didn't want to hear about the riots; they wanted as little as possible to do with the riots.'[3]

While interviewing people in Notting Hill or Nottingham the question was occasionally put to me: 'Why rake it all up? Why not let sleeping dogs lie?' I fully understand this sentiment. The riots caused misery to countless individuals, black and white, many of whom have tried to blot out the memory. As Pansy Jeffrey, who came to Britain from British Guiana in the 1940s and who was appointed as a specialist West Indian welfare worker in Notting Hill after the riots, put it: 'It was a time to live through, a time to forget.'[4]

Without wishing to re-open old wounds, I have tried to draw on individuals' feelings and recollections in order to breathe life into the past events of 1958. Much has been written in recent years on the causes and dynamics of racism, and our understanding of the structural forces behind it – ideology, race and class, the imperial past – have been enriched in consequence. But often what is lacking from these accounts is the aspect of how impersonal forces impinge on and distort the lives of individuals. What I have attempted in this book is to link the structural with the individual, with Notting Hill and the riots acting as the focus.

I have chosen to concentrate on Notting Hill because it was the scene of the worst rioting in 1958. Although this gives a consciously local dimension to the book, many of the issues I describe in relation to Notting Hill could equally be applied elsewhere. Rioting also occurred concurrently in Nottingham; I have included references to these events more as a point of comparison with Notting Hill than as a comprehensive account. Apart from newspaper reports, government records and literature from the time, much of the material for this book is drawn from an extensive series of interviews I conducted in 1983 and 1988 with residents, both white and black, who lived through the riots. On a point of terminology, I have opted for the term 'West Indians' to describe black people from the Caribbean rather than 'Afro-Caribbean'. I felt that this is in keeping with the spirit of the 1950s when the latter term had not yet been coined.

1988, the thirtieth anniversary of the riots, is an appropriate year to uncover what lies beneath the public amnesia. The story of the 1958 riots illustrates much about English society which we might still prefer to forget. The lessons to be learnt are still relevant today; indeed, perhaps more so now than they have ever been.

I would like to thank the following for their advice and assistance: Susan Benson, Aggrey Burke, Brian Curle and the Kensington Library local studies section, Tony Gould, Stuart Hall, Guy Martin, Sylvia Mulvey, the North Kensington Local History Project, Dave Randall, former vicar of St Clement's church Notting Dale, Carole Rudkin and the pensioners' club of the Nottingham Afro-Caribbean Association ACNA, Richard Silburn of Nottingham University, Aubrey Singer and Ronnie Benjamin of the BBC and the BBC film and video library, A. Sivanandan and the Institute of Race Relations, Ruth Spence, Gareth Stedman Jones, and Bernadine Wray. I am particularly grateful to Christina Dunhill, Ken Leech, John Western and Monica Whitlock for their invaluable comments and to my editor Iradj Bagherzade. Above all, Baron Baker, Peter Fryer and Jessica Morris have sustained me with their constant advice, encouragement and support.

My special thanks are reserved for those people who have shared their memories so generously with me: Ron Burnel, Donald Chesworth, George Clark, Frank Critchlow, Police Constable Bob Davis*, King Dick, Frances Ezzrecco, John*, Margaret* and Martin Garrett*, Harold Gayle, John Howe, Pansy Jeffrey, Chris Lemaitre, Jean Maggs, David Mason, Owen McFarlane, Mary O'Connor and Margery Bonfield, Horace Ove, George Powe, Samuel Roberts*, Harold Spencer*, Peter Taylor*, Viola Taylor, Jim Wright*, Ivo de Souza, Ivan Weekes, and John Wray. The asterisks indicate where I have used pseudonyms to protect the privacy of individuals. I hope that all these people feel that I have done justice to what is, after all, their own story.

Edward Pilkington
April 1988

Introduction

Early one Sunday morning at the end of August, 1958, Baron Baker, a Jamaican living in west London, was woken by the telephone. He was told there was trouble in Notting Hill, an area with a large black community less than a mile from his flat. Baker took the note of urgency in his friend's voice with a pinch of salt. 'I thought he meant a couple of lads were being silly, and having a little skirmish.' He dressed unhurriedly and went down to the street.

Outside, the sun was already high and the air was thick and hazy, a dense mixture of the heat and dust that covered this decaying part of London. Baker decided to walk to clear his head, cutting across the Harrow Road and into the top of Ladbroke Grove which runs through the centre of Notting Hill. As he strolled down the Grove, passing rows of elegant but dilapidated houses, he began to feel that there was, indeed, something wrong. There was unusual movement for a Sunday morning, when most people were normally in bed or at church. People stood at street corners – young white people, mostly men, some wearing the Teddy Boy jackets and drainpipe trousers which were then in fashion. They looked ill-at-ease. Then Baron Baker spotted motor bike chains hung like beads around their necks. Some of the men held iron bars or chunks of wood, swinging them idly from hand to hand; others brandished long, sharpened steel knives. Baker was in no hurry to ask them what they were doing – he already knew: 'I could tell that this time it was the real thing.'[1]

Turning quickly off Ladbroke Grove into one of the side-streets that led west, he paused to collect his thoughts. He remembered hearing about a party in Blechynden Street the night before, so he made his way there, walking fast but trying to look nonchalant so as to avoid attracting attention. Clusters of white people threw whistles and jeers in his direction, but more in bravado than as a serious challenge and nobody tried to stop him. When he reached the two-storey house in Blechynden Street where the party had been held he was amazed to find every window in the building smashed and the front door hanging off its hinges. Inside, the Jamaican who had held the party, King Dick, was sitting amidst a sea of broken glass and splintered furniture. 'They came and smashed the place up,' he said.[2]

It all began with a young Swedish woman, Majbritt Morrison, who lived with her West Indian husband, Raymond, near Blechynden Street. On that Saturday night she had been dancing at King Dick's party, but left shortly before closing time, not wanting to walk home too late. Recently her neighbours had been calling her offensive names and bricks had been thrown through the windows of her house.

As she turned into Bramley Road, she saw a large crowd of white people milling around. At first she thought they were drinking outside the pubs to enjoy the summer heat but as she got closer she became apprehensive. Most of the people in the street were men and they looked decidedly angry. She detected some of her neighbours among them and they recognised her. One teenager standing on the edge of the crowd pointed at her: 'There's another one, another black man's trollop!' Suddenly, the crowd turned towards her, shouting 'White trash!' 'Nigger lover!' 'Get her! Kill her!'

Majbritt Morrison was not one to be intimidated by a pack of aggressive men. As she approached the crowd she kept her eyes fixed straight ahead, knowing better than to turn her back, and continued striding down the middle of the street, ignoring the verbal onslaught and ducking milk bottles and chunks of wood. Outside her house she was greeted by police cars and fire engines, their beacons flashing; smoke was pouring from her ground floor room where a petrol bomb had been thrown through the window. Police officers met her on the steps and told her to get inside but she refused, turning on the crowd which now surrounded her house. At first she tried pleading with them not to start anything, but when they responded with jeers and yet more abuse she exploded: 'Is it blood you want? Go on then, KILL ME!' Someone took her at her word and she felt a piercing pain in her back. 'I saw one of the boys standing there with a big iron bar with which he had hit me. I nearly fainted but I wouldn't let anyone see how much it really hurt, so I stood up again.' This time the police stepped in and grabbed her, pushing her forcefully into the house.[3]

Once Morrison had been removed from its grasp the crowd – now over 200 strong – descended on King Dick's party in Blechynden Street. By this time the house was full of revellers and a sounds system was playing, with Count Suckle – one of the first black sounds men in London – acting as disc jockey. King Dick remembers that a calypso record called 'Oriental Ball' was playing when he heard a buzzing noise, like a swarm of bees. He went outside and there, coming towards him, was the crowd. He watched, stunned, as hundreds of people approached. Then suddenly bricks and iron bars started smashing through the windows, the white crowd chanting 'Kill the niggers!' 'Keep Britain White!'

That was the start of four consecutive days and nights of race riots in Notting Hill, some of the worst outbreaks of civil unrest and racial violence in Britain this century. Black people were chased down back streets and beaten up; some were put in hospital, others had their houses fire-bombed. White people descended on Notting Hill from all over west London to 'see the niggers run' and when West Indians took steps to protect themselves, pitched battles raged between whites and blacks. Outside London, fighting also erupted in Nottingham where white crowds up to 4,000 strong swarmed around the St Ann's area near the city centre, 'nigger hunting'.

For West Indians, the riots marked the culmination of ten years' experience of living and working in Britain. Although black people have lived here since the third century AD,[4] from 1948 West Indians began arriving in Britain in unprecedented numbers. Between 1951 and 1958 an estimated 125,000 West Indians came to Britain.[5] As a result, more white Britons came in contact with black people than ever before, especially in the industrial centres of London, Nottingham, Birmingham and Manchester.

The arrival of the newcomers opened up a debate about the status of black people within Britain. Sociologists deliberated over how long it would take the West Indians to become fully 'integrated' in the white 'host' society. Other commentators asked whether Britain would develop a 'colour problem' similar to that of the American South.[6] Both the Attlee and then successive Conservative governments engaged in confidential discussions on the issue of black immigration. At the start of the decade they focused their attentions on the question of whether or not to import black workers in order to ease Britain's post-war labour shortage. In 1956 this issue was resolved in favour of recruiting West Indians for work in British services and industries. But while Ministers were concerned to satisfy growing demands for labour, they were also preoccupied about the effects of an influx of black people on the 'British Way of Life'. For many Cabinet Ministers, a multi-racial society was not an ideal of harmony to be striven for, but a spectre to be courted at Britain's peril. Ironically, just when West Indians began to be actively recruited and brought into the country in 1956, the Conservative Government finalised plans to recast Britain's nationality laws in order to keep black people out.

While the Government was privately consumed by these preoccupations, publicly it adopted a *laissez-faire* attitude towards the West Indians. No assistance was provided to facilitate their entry into British society and no attempt was made to inform the general public about who the new arrivals were or where they had come from. Consequently, white people developed their own theories about the West Indians based primarily on hearsay and conjecture. Although many whites set eyes on blacks for the first time in the 1950s, they already held strong preconceptions about their racial characteristics. Blacks were regarded as unskilled, poorly educated, lazy and stupid, but blessed with extraordinary sexual powers.

These prejudices affected the way white people related to the newcomers. Landlords would not accept black lodgers because they were thought to be dirty, or because the neighbours would object; employers refused to take on black workers because they assumed them to be lazy and unreliable; and trade unions resisted the entry of black people into factories because they were suspected of undermining pay and working conditions.

Through the combination of ignorant prejudice and conscious racial discrimination, the 'host' community obliged the West Indians to take the lowliest and worst-paid jobs and to live in the most run-down parts of London such as Notting Hill. This west London area was dilapidated and overcrowded in the 1950s, with unprotected tenancies under the control of racketeering landlords, including the most notorious Peter Rachman. Forced into Rachman's properties because few other landlords would accept them, the West Indians paid exorbitant rents in exchange for squalid box rooms.

The sight of black people living in overcrowded hovels was proof in the eyes of Notting Hill's white residents that West Indians were dirty and primitive. Racial animosities were particularly intense in that part of Notting Hill where Blechynden Street is located: Notting Dale. This working-class neighbourhood maintained a primarily white popula-tion throughout the 1950s, and was renowned locally for its strong sense of community – hostile towards outsiders. By 1958, when moderate unemployment aggravated Notting Dale's economic insecurities, racial hostility had begun to be expressed through violence. Fascist organisations such as Oswald Mosley's Union Movement provided the spark which lit the fuse.

The riots marked the end of an era. They shattered the West Indians' belief in Britain as the Mother Country and in their own status as British citizens. They now felt like strangers in a land which they had regarded as their second home and although they still had British passports, it was as if their British citizenship had been stripped from them. In its place, black people began searching for a new self-identity modelled on their common Afro-Caribbean roots.

The ten years from 1948 to 1958 were formative in the development of modern Britain's race relations, and many of today's conflicts and challenges stem directly from them. The events recounted here form the opening chapter to a story which is still unfolding.

1
Exodus to the Mother Country

On 22 June 1948 a British freighter, the *Empire Windrush*, an old troop-carrier, slid upstream with the tide between the narrowing shores of Kent and Essex, bound for Tilbury Docks.[1] Five hundred Jamaicans, mostly men, lined the railings on the upper deck, peering out over green fields that stretched as far as the horizon. It was the last leg of a journey which had brought them from Kingston, via Mexico and Bermuda, across five thousand miles of Atlantic ocean. With more passengers on board than berths, many had been forced to lay their heads wherever they could find a bare plank.

But despite their exhaustion and the British fog that greeted them, nothing could hide the West Indians' exhilaration at finally arriving in England. Several of them had served in the RAF during the war and were eager to take up life in England where they had left off three years earlier. Having played their part in defeating Hitler they were coming back to reap the benefits. Others were setting eyes on this green and pleasant land for the first time. Nevertheless, they too regarded this as a return journey. Some people called Britain their second home, others the 'Mother Country'.[2]

Britain could hardly have been more different from the islands they had left behind. The smoggy grey streets of London replaced sun-drenched Caribbean landscapes. Everyday objects which British people took for granted were a source of amazement and amusement for them. 'I couldn't believe it when I saw houses with smoke belching out of them. I thought: What a lot of factories! And someone else said, "My God! These houses are on fire!" We'd never seen chimneys before.'[3]

But although so much was different, the British Caribbean and its 'Mother Country' had been inextricably linked ever since merchants first began shipping African slaves to the West Indies in the seventeenth century. The West Indians' slave ancestors had played a crucial role in the development of Britain's mercantile prosperity, as part of the highly lucrative triangular trading arrangement between England, Africa and the Caribbean. From the seventeenth century, ships left British ports laden with textiles, metal-work, beer and miscellaneous luxuries. On the African coast these commodities were bartered for slaves who were then shipped across the Atlantic. Those who survived the notorious middle passage were exchanged for sugar, spices, molasses, rum and tobacco which were in turn brought back to Britain. Some of the accumulated profits were ploughed back into buying more manufactured goods and so the cycle began again.[4]

In 1948 Britain still ruled directly over the Caribbean islands. The largest sugar plantations in Jamaica, Trinidad, Barbados and the rest of the British West Indies were still owned by Creole families of English descent. Public administration was also controlled by expatriates. Although colonial service was no longer as prestigious as it had been during the heyday of the Empire, it remained an obvious career move for English graduates and they continued to monopolise the higher grades of the Caribbean civil service.

Torn from their African heritage by English merchants, the slaves and their free descendants attached themselves to the only cultural values at hand. These they learnt at school and through contact with expatriates, under the title of the 'British Way of Life' – a sanitised version of British society and manners which was made to appear the very height of excellence. It was like a bottled version of British society with all the bitterness taken out – an export draft which tasted very sweet compared with the home brew.

Moreover it was a potent concoction and under its influence West Indians formed the impression that the Mother Country was the greatest civilisation in the world – the seat of law and order, justice and democracy. They believed England was a country where everyone spoke with an upper-class accent. 'The image I was taught was that the English spoke perfectly,' says Ivan Weekes who comes from Barbados which used to be called 'Little England'. 'They were all well bred and brought up because they owned half the world.'[5]

By the 1950s most school teachers in the Caribbean were black. English men and women only filled the highest posts in the most select schools. Nevertheless, teachers continued to direct the thoughts of their pupils in the direction of the Mother Country. The curriculum was taken lock, stock and barrel from English text books. In history lessons, West Indian children were taught about English monarchs and noblemen, but nothing about the slave trade or the black experience in the Caribbean. 'I can tell you the names and dates of every king and queen of England,' says Pansy Jeffrey from British Guiana (now Guyana).[6] In geography they learnt by heart the mountain ranges and rivers of the Mother Country, not of their own islands; they studied Shakespeare and Milton and struggled with Latin grammar; and at the end of the year they took exams set by the school boards of Oxford and Cambridge.[7] Even in the professions – the civil service, medicine, law – only English qualifications were accepted and students who could afford higher education had to come to England.[8]

The message was clear: Caribbean people should be grateful for the fact that Britain was ruling over them because until they had learnt how to conduct themselves according to the unwritten laws of the British Way of Life they would be unable to govern themselves. 'We were taught at school that we were descended from primitive African tribes,' remembers Baron Baker, 'who were uncivilised and ungodly until the British arrived and carried them out of the wilderness.'[9]

Children were also taught to thank the English for having liberated them. Every year, on 1st August, the West Indies celebrated carnival. This was a time of great rejoicing, of colour and gaiety just as it is today, marking the date in 1833 when Queen Victoria gave her assent to the Act of Parliament abolishing slavery. But carnival was not a celebration of having thrown off the white man's yoke. On the contrary, it was a day when the British Empire was adulated even more intensely than usual.

In his memoirs the Jamaican broadcaster George Spence recalls his first carnival in August Town in the late 1920s. The procession was led by a man in a multi-coloured costume walking on stilts representing the legendary liberated slave, John Kanu. As the procession wound its way through the town accompanied by drums, guitars and bamboo fifes, adults clapped their hands and sang songs of slavery and emancipation. 'Merrily, merrily I dance and sing / Queen Victoria set me free.'[10]

Another important day in the calendar was Empire Day on 24th May. Organisers were sent round all the schools to conduct rehearsals of 'Rule Britannia', 'Men of Harlech' and other patriotic British songs. Then on the big day hundreds of children were lined up along the walls of the civic centre in each parish. In George Spence's case this was Manchester, Jamaica. Each child was given a Union Jack and as the local Salvation Army struck up a rousing tune the children were marched down the main road to the town square where they were lectured by white men and women standing on a platform. They were the proud members of the greatest Empire on earth, they were told: they were little Britons. When the speeches were over they rendered 'Rule Britannia' to the satisfaction of the white organisers, but the evident dissatisfaction of the black teachers, who slapped them and told them to sing up. The organisers handed out bags of chocolates, sweets and cakes. 'I waved my little Union Jack with one hand, took a bite from the chocolates in the other, and naturally enough became convinced that the Union Jack and good things went together.'[11]

One of the central pillars of the British Way of Life was the idea that the British treated people equally according to the rule of law. West Indians were taught that if they respected the British, the British would respect them. The idea was that the British judged everybody on their individual merits and did not discriminate against anyone on religious, political or racial grounds. Certainly, Britain's handling of her colonies compared favourably with the systematic racial segregation that was practised in the American South. By the Second World War West Indian blacks had gained a foothold within lower administrative grades of the local civil service and within government. Jamaica, for instance, had been granted a new constitution in 1944 which introduced a lower chamber elected through universal suffrage. White expatriates still dominated politically, but they had a reputation for being enlightened and benevolent rulers with good manners, who respected black West Indian people.

But one only had to scratch below the surface to find racial discrimination. The most select hotels were reserved for white guests. Even the eminent Sir Frank McDavid from British Guiana was refused a room in a hotel in Bermuda in 1953 because he was black. The Secretary of State for the Colonies, Oliver Lyttleton, was questioned on this matter back in Westminster. His reply was that although Her Majesty's Government strongly opposed any colour bar he was 'advised that its maintenance in certain hotels is essential to the tourist trade on which the people of the Colony as a whole depend for their livelihood.'[12]

It was implicitly understood that the British Way of Life meant the White Way of Life. Michael de Freitas, who lived in Notting Hill at the time of the race riots and who went on to become an influential figure in the British Black Power movement in the 1960s as Michael X, was brought up by his mother in Trinidad to think that white was pretty, black ugly. De Freitas was prevented from mixing with children who had darker skins than his own, or from doing things that 'black boys did'. He had to sneak out of the house whenever he wanted to join his friends on long walks into the rolling hills behind Port of Spain, picking mangoes and guava and catching tropical fish. 'She wanted me to be a little white boy because she didn't make it to be a white lady.'[13]

The West Indian population was multi-racial. In the schools English, Afro-Caribbean, Chinese, Asian, Portuguese, Latin American and Syrian children were taught together.[14] But although there was no segregation, and little racial hostility, class was still defined along relatively clear racial lines. As a member of the League of Coloured Peoples – a London-based black pressure group – put it in 1943: 'In the British Empire there can be no Negro Governor because the maintenance of white prestige is considered to be an essential pillar of the imperial regime, and Negroes are not allowed, except when it cannot be helped, into administrative posts of distinction and responsibility.'[15] In the wider community whites formed the *élite*, then came Syrians and Chinese, next black Afro-Caribbeans. Asians were generally at the bottom of the pecking order – they were called 'coolies' and the saying was 'Two coolies make one person.'[16]

The belief in British equality was reinforced by comparison with America. West Indians had first-hand experience of white American attitudes to race during the war. Baron Baker's first taste of military life was in the American airbase in Sandy Gully, Jamaica, where he was surprised to find that West Indians appeared to be regarded as a threat. They ate in separate canteens while armed American soldiers kept guard and on pay day machine guns were trained on them as they queued up to collect their wages. Baker concluded that the British Way of Life was infinitely preferable to that of the Americans. Later, when he had the opportunity of cutting cane in America he declined the offer and signed up instead for the British Air Force.[17]

Some West Indians volunteered to fight for the Mother Country right at the start of the war, paying their own passage. At first the British Government resisted the idea of black British citizens joining the ranks of commissioned officers. Later, however, it modified its stance by offering black people from the colonies 'emergency' commissions for the duration of the war. But this was not enough to satisfy Harold Moody, the Jamaican president of the League of Coloured Peoples. Moody explained that it was illogical to give commissions only for the duration. If the principle is accepted now, he said, surely it must be acceptable all the time.[18] Under the League's pressure, the Government agreed to open all ranks of the armed forces to black people and two of Moody's children rose to the rank of major.

By 1942 Britain was desperately in need of more workers and the Labour War Cabinet member, Ernest Bevin, began a powerful recruitment drive within the West Indies. Volunteers were sought through newspapers, posters and government publications. Altogether over 8,000 West Indians were brought to England by the RAF as ground crew – mainly as flight mechanics – and another 345 served as technicians in munitions factories in Liverpool and other industrial towns, so releasing white working-class conscripts for active service.[19]

While serving in Britain, the West Indians were confronted by racial hostility, especially from white American GIs. In March 1942 a West Indian was attacked near a Lyons tea-house in London by two white US Marines, one armed with a knife. In Liverpool the West Indian technicians were constantly harassed by American soldiers. The manager of a casino in Warrington imposed a colour bar in 1943 after receiving a request from an American captain who wrote: 'It is not our intention to dictate the policies of privately owned establishments. But in the interests of eliminating the trouble in which our troops may be involved we will appreciate your co-operation in prohibiting negroes from attending the dances.'[20] This provoked a storm of protest from the West Indians, some of whom threatened to go on strike. As British subjects they were understandably indignant when dance hall owners bowed to the segregation policies of the American army. There was little or no colour bar in their own countries, they said, and they asked the Government why it had done nothing to resist the Americans' demands.

Ivo de Souza, one of the first Jamaicans to join the RAF, spent part of the war years working as a West Indian welfare officer. He remembers that although the most unfortunate men were those garrisoned near American troops, West Indians were also harassed in pubs and dance halls by English men and women.[21] The West Indian technicians working as civilians in the munitions factories had the worst experiences. White workers in the Havilland Aircraft Company in Bolton threatened, in February 1943, to walk out in protest against the employment of 28 black people, which they argued would be in 'undue proportion' to the total workforce of 6,000.[22] West Indian women also had to cope with abuse. A black woman in the ATS was reportedly refused a new issue of shoes by her officer who said: 'At home you don't wear shoes anyway.'[23]

Although West Indians had to put up with harassment and prejudice, general recollection of the war is favourable. 'The war years were good years for us. I have no regrets about

them at all.'[24] Harsh military discipline helped to quash any
nascent racial antagonism. Those servicemen who might have
been tempted to bait black people may have hesitated because
they knew that rowdy behaviour would be severely punished.
The military regime also opened up promotion opportunities for
black servicemen which would have been closed in the outside
world. Although the West Indians were initially trained in
separate units, they were quickly incorporated into mixed
squadrons and given equal rights and duties, and many
rose rapidly within the ranks. Ivo de Souza excelled and
was promoted to full Squadron Leader. Success stories such
as his not only provided an inspiring example for other
West Indians but also fostered respect among their white
colleagues.

While the West Indian servicemen were fighting for Britain,
the economic situation back in the Caribbean was deteriorating
rapidly. The West Indies were devastated by the war and the
interruption in world trade. Almost entirely dependent on sugar
exports, the Caribbean economies suffered immensely from
wartime austerity and the collapse in commodity prices. The
cost of living almost doubled during the war and real incomes
fell drastically. In Jamaica unemployment rose to over 25 per
cent of the workforce and many of the remaining jobs were
seasonal or part time. Average per capita incomes were £52
per year, compared with £200 in Britain and £400 in the
United States.[25]

As the war drew to a close the West Indians in Britain
grew increasingly anxious about returning to poverty and
unemployment. The 350 civilian technicians were particularly
alarmed as they were the first to be demobilised. Many tried
desperately to stay on. Sixty-five technicians wrote in September
1945 to George Hall MP, Secretary of State for the Colonies,
expressing their concern.

> On the eve of the general repatriation, we the Jamaican
> technicians, do respectfully beg to be considered for post-war
> work. It is the feeling of us that we are only going home to swell
> the ranks of the unemployed that have already reached alarming
> proportions. Our chances of procuring jobs are not only doubtful
> but in reality chanceless. We have served this country to the best

of our ability in order that the greatest empire in the world should be preserved. We think it is only fair that work should be provided for us so that we would win the peace. We do not ask for special facilities, but just a reward for our part in winning the war.[26]

Their plea fell on deaf ears. As the war came to an end, the Ministry of Labour prepared to repatriate them and as early as April 1945 officials in the Ministry began making arrangements for demobilisation.

The general impression is that not more than 50 per cent of the West Indians want to return home at all. As they are British subjects we cannot force them to return, but it would be undesirable to encourage them to remain in this country. We should therefore take immediate advantage of every expression in favour of repatriation as the longer the men stay here, the less ready they will be to go.[27]

Only the most obstinate stayed on. The others grudgingly accepted the British Government's offer of a free boat ride home. As they watched the English coastline gradually disappear into the horizon, their grievances against Britain seemed to fade away, to be replaced by a cloud of nostalgia. By the time they arrived in the Caribbean, many were already planning to get back to the Mother Country at the earliest opportunity.

By 1948 many of the ex-servicemen had saved up the boat fare that would carry them back across the Atlantic. Early in the year a rumour began to spread in Jamaica that the *Empire Windrush* would soon be arriving in Kingston, discharging its cargo from the Middle East, and then embarking for Britain. This was confirmed in the national daily *The Gleaner* which carried advertisements for passages at £28 10s., about a third of the usual commercial rate.[28] When the *Empire Windrush* docked in Kingston, ironically on Empire Day, hundreds of people thronged the quayside and many had to be turned away.

Of the *Empire Windrush*'s 500 passengers, eighteen were stowaways, including the only woman on board. About one third were war veterans. The rest were leaving their birthplace for the unknown, partly in the hope that it would provide an escape from economic hardship and a means to self-betterment, and partly as an expedition to their Mother Country. 'England was home in the mind of every small boy in the West Indies when I was growing up,' wrote Michael de Freitas, ' "Land of hope and glory." We sang that song as little boys with the greatest fervour. I was thrilled with the prospect of seeing the Mother Country.'[29]

The arrival of the *Empire Windrush* provoked a state of near panic within the Attlee Labour Government. Officials had only been warned about the West Indians' arrival two weeks before the ship was due and senior civil servants and politicians from the Ministry of Labour and the Colonial Office were thrown into a frenzy of correspondence. Letters were flung from one end of Whitehall to the other as each Ministry tried to convince the other of its responsibility for the newcomers.

The Colonial Office argued that the West Indians did not fall within its remit because they had already left the colonies, and urged the Ministry of Labour to act in the interests of Commonwealth relations. Lord Listowel from the Colonial Office argued that:

> They are British subjects (some, at any rate, ex-servicemen) and we can neither prevent their landing nor compel their departure. We must therefore see that the smoothest possible arrangements are made to minimise the risk of any undesirable incidents or complaints that the Mother Country does not bother to look after Coloured Colonial British subjects.[30]

Officials in the Ministry of Labour replied that West Indians came to Britain of their own free will and could not expect to be looked after. But on this occasion the Colonial Office won the debate and the Ministry of Labour had to accept the task of providing the West Indians with temporary accommodation and help with finding jobs. The Labour Minister, Sir George Isaacs, made it clear that he did not intend to set a precedent, however.

> The arrival of these substantial numbers of men under no organised arrangement is bound to result in considerable difficulty and disappointment. I have no knowledge of their qualifications or capacities and can give no assurance that they can be found suitable work. I hope no encouragement will be given to others to follow their example.[31]

This provoked an angry response from political leaders in Barbados who said his attitude was 'not calculated to promote loyalty and affection on the part of British citizens in the Caribbean.'[32]

In the following week, Isaacs circulated an internal memorandum within the Ministry arguing that the West Indians should not be offered accommodation in government hostels because that would be treating 'those men very much more favourably than our own people in this country, and furthermore it would undoubtedly, we think, encourage a further influx.'[33] But there were few alternatives, and the Ministry was forced to write to the government-run National Service Hostels Corporation in Connaught Place, London, requesting beds. It received a pointed reply from the Corporation's executive director, R.H. Blindloss:

> I hope whatever happens that it will not eventually be decided that they should be put into any of our hostels. We have had some experience of dealing with Jamaicans. I cannot say that the experience we have had makes one anxious to extend it for, of all the differing types of people and nationalities who come to us as residents, the most provocative trouble-makers have been the West Indians.[34]

In the end, however, the Corporation acquiesced, saying that if the Government was foolhardy enough to let the West Indians into the country, it would house them – but only up to a maximum of three per hostel.[35]

Under this restriction there would not be enough hostel beds to accommodate all the West Indians. The only alternative that could be found was the Clapham Deep Shelter in south London, an old wartime air-raid shelter formed out of a lateral extension to an Underground line. The bomb shelter was re-opened and half the West Indians on board the *Empire Windrush*, those without addresses to go to, moved in. There they stayed for three weeks in cramped conditions which an official described as 'far from ideal for a stay of more than 72 hours.'[36]

During their sojourn in Clapham Common the Mayor of the nearby borough of Lambeth, Jack Simpson, held a party at the town hall in their honour. The Labour MP, Marcus Lipton, urged them to regard Lambeth as their second home; and partly because of this good will, a black community was born in Brixton.[37]

At the same time, the West Indians had their first experiences of looking for employment and housing in Britain. They had been warned that they might have difficulties by the Colonial Office which had despatched J.H.Smythe, an African flight lieutenant, to talk to them on board the *Empire Windrush*. 'I could not honestly paint you a very rosy picture of your future in Britain,' he said. But he assured them that if they were 'serious minded' and prepared to work hard they could make their way.[38] There was good reason for Smythe's note of caution. A few of the West Indians lodged in the Clapham Shelter had difficulty finding other accommodation.[39] Others had trouble getting work. Fifty of the ex-servicemen re-joined the RAF and the rest went looking for jobs across the country, mainly in the industrial centres where the technicians had worked in munitions factories during the war – Birmingham, Nottingham, Leicester, Lancashire, South Wales and even as far as Scotland.[40]

This was an extremely inauspicious start to post-war black settlement in Britain. Once the West Indians had left Clapham Common the Government washed its hands of them. The Ministry of Labour expressed its relief that they had dispersed to different parts of the country where 'even though they did not get immediate employment, they would cease to be recognisable as a problem.'[41]

2
An Expendable Commodity

'When I left the Caribbean I felt I was coming to a paradise, like Alice in Wonderland,' recalls Trinidadian Horace Ove who came to Britain in the late 1950s. But when Ove passed through Customs he found a world quite divorced from his expectations. He was shocked by how old and grubby the streets were and how dim the street lights. At night smog would descend on London, reducing visibility to five yards and making one's eyes smart. It struck Ove that everybody dressed in black or grey, as though they were at a funeral. 'Then it suddenly hit me what I had left behind and where I had come to.'[1]

It was not only that London was drab in comparison with the image of the imperial capital that the West Indians had grown up with. The weather was cold and damp and, moreover, many found being thrown among a white population a traumatic experience. Ivan Weekes remembers: 'The first shock was being canoodled up into a little room with another person. It was quite shattering. It was an affront to the sense of space I had grown accustomed to. I felt claustrophobic, trapped. Then the cold! It was more than I had possibly imagined. Nobody spoke to me when I said good morning and then a sea of white faces hit me.'[2]

Horace Ove was surprised when he heard a taxi driver's cockney accent. 'I couldn't understand a damn word when the cabby started speaking to me. In the Caribbean I had only had contact with gentlemen and the upper classes.' He was also amazed by the sight of English manual labourers. In the West Indies menial work was performed almost exclusively by Afro-Caribbeans or Asians. But here, for the first time, West Indians came face to face with porters, road sweepers and dustbin collectors who were white.[3]

A popular belief in the 1950s was that most West Indians were poorly educated agricultural labourers: a theory which was propounded even in Parliament. In 1958 the Earl of Swinton told the House of Lords that the great majority of West Indians coming to Britain were unskilled. Or as a local London newspaper put it, England was becoming the 'dumping ground for the world's riff-raff'.[4]

In fact, it is estimated that 24 per cent of the West Indians coming to Britain had professional or managerial experience, 46 per cent were skilled workers, 5 per cent semi-skilled and only 13 per cent unskilled manual workers.[5] A very wide range of professions were reflected among the passengers on board the *Empire Windrush*: masons, mechanics, journalists, students, musicians, boxers and even cyclists attending an international competition.[6] Many of the ex-servicemen who returned to Britain had spent five years in the RAF learning and practising skills that would have equipped them for virtually any job in mechanics on the market. Moreover, most were in their twenties, and they all spoke English. Indeed, the West Indies were losing some of the cream of their labour force.[7]

Unskilled West Indians had no difficulty finding manual jobs in factories or services. However, the skilled workers who expected to find work equivalent to their abilities were largely disappointed. Horace Ove came hoping to study interior design with a firm of architects, a profession for which his experience as an artist made him particularly suitable. He carried a letter of introduction from an English architect whom he had met in the West Indies, recommending him to a firm in London. But when he arrived there he was told: 'We don't employ people like you.' This bald statement was offered without explanation or elaboration. Ove was stunned. 'That was my first experience of racism in Britain.'[8]

People with similar skills got equally short shrift from employers. Teachers, carpenters, mechanics, tailors, doctors and journalists were all turned away. Sometimes excuses were given: the West Indians were over-qualified or under-qualified or even both. Electricians would be rebuffed because although they were fully qualified they were said to be incapable of supervising other staff, and then told they were not suitable for even the lowest paid work because they were too highly qualified. The shock of rejection was particularly disturbing for ex-servicemen, who had been accustomed in the armed forces to the principle that diligence would be rewarded. They naturally assumed that a similar meritocracy would operate within civilian society.

George Powe fought in the RAF during the war and says that in uniform he was usually welcomed and treated with respect. But when he returned from Jamaica to Britain as a civilian in 1950 and went to live in Nottingham he found that the skills he had learnt during the war were virtually useless. When he went for an interview at a local engineering factory he wasn't even allowed through the gates – a woman shouted down from a window that there were no jobs going for 'his sort'. Powe complained to the manager and to his surprise was taken on; but less than two months later he was back outside the gates again. The same manager had sacked him because he thought Powe was becoming too familiar with a white female employee. Later Powe acquired teacher training qualifications, but this didn't help much. He couldn't even get work on the buses because he was told he was not fit for the job and one company turned him away because they said his hands were too rough.[9]

Baron Baker was one of the few West Indian servicemen to stay on at the end of the war. It was only after he had been demobilised that he began to realise just how prejudiced English people could be. 'When I left the Air Force I started to find that the English were racist. Trying to get a job on a bus as a conductor was unheard of. They never dreamed of giving a black man a job there.'[10]

Employers were not all straightforwardly racist, however. Many were ambivalent in their attitude towards West Indians, being primarily concerned to maintain production, and in the labour-starved 1950s any extra pair of hands was welcomed. On the other hand, employers were not indifferent to racial distinctions between workers and some had been influenced by colonial service. A factory boss who had learnt his trade managing Jamaica's bauxite mines, where black men and women worked long hours in poor conditions for little pay, would not necessarily be the most enlightened employer of black workers back in Britain. Most employers had never lived or worked abroad, but they still often held dogmatic views about black people. They were susceptible to the caricature of West Indians as unskilled illiterates who were only fit for the kind of jobs that no one else would take: dirty, poorly paid jobs that were either seasonal or took place in unsocial hours. Blacks, it was felt, could not be trusted with positions of responsibility and should not be given a high profile within the business.[11]

Employers also speculated about their customers' views. Until the 1960s, when shops first began employing black women on their counters, no West Indians were permitted to work in positions where they came in contact with the public because it was feared that customers would withdraw their trade. This fear was thought to justify the imposition of a colour bar. One manufacturer, described as one of the younger, more progressive employers explained that, 'One is in business after all. The public wouldn't stand for it.' Another was more apologetic: 'I know it is a terrible thing to say, but colour prejudice does exist, and it is a risk we dare not take.' Neither of them had actually gauged their customers' feelings through opinion polls or market research.[12]

Similar arguments were employed in the building trade. A common objection to black builders was that white women clients would not feel safe at home in the presence of a black man.[13] A survey conducted in the 1950s into employers' views, focusing on the building industry in Stepney in east London, found that some employers genuinely welcomed black workers and went out of their way to encourage, train and support them. However, other firms refused outright to employ blacks and over 80 per cent only took blacks as a last resort. Many said they looked forward to the return of unemployment which would allow them to engage a totally white labour force.[14]

The West Indians were said to fight among themselves and to have a 'persecution complex', reacting to any criticism as though it were racially motivated. Blacks also had a reputation for being transient workers, even though the turnover of employees was as high among whites. Some employers were more emotive in their appraisal of West Indians, complaining that they were dirty, lazy, greedy for the highest rates of pay, threatening and abusive. If it was necessary to employ blacks to make up the workforce, these employers advocated splitting them up within the company. 'It's the same with the Irish. If you take in certain minorities they stick together and if you have too many, the worst influences prevail. If they are isolated and put to work on their own they get ahead.'[15]

Fears about the reactions of white employees were also voiced. An employer told the Stepney survey that he had decided to stop taking on blacks because his white employees disliked their body odour.[16] Another said that he welcomed West Indians, but he would never promote them to charge-hands because his white workers would not tolerate it. Employers seemed particularly anxious on this score where white women were involved. 'It's asking for trouble if you have any female labour – not because the coloured men misbehave but because the girls and the white chaps believe they might.'[17]

Employers had reason to be concerned about their white workers, who were in a position of considerable power in the early 1950s due to the scarcity of labour. Threats of strikes and walk-outs were taken very seriously and avoided at all costs. Employers feared that if their industries saw an influx of black workers they might lose their long-established white labour. The owner of a large building firm said: 'I consider that the criterion here is not so much the quality of the individual so much as his acceptability amongst the existing staff. Refusal might be disastrous.'[18]

The 1950s were, in fact, punctuated by a number of industrial disputes over the issue of black employment. In West Bromwich a major struggle between unions and management erupted in February 1955 over the recruitment of the first non-European bus conductor, Bhikha Patel. His appointment triggered the most complete stoppage of transport in West Bromwich since the 1926 General Strike. In other circumstances Patel might have regarded that as quite an achievement. But this strike was motivated by a desire to ensure that the buses remained a white bastion, and it was directed personally against him – or rather the colour of his skin.[19]

The all-out call was honoured by every bus worker in West Bromwich – Patel was the only person to cross the picket lines – and the strike even had the support of neighbouring transport workers. The Birmingham Transport Corporation, although it had already allowed blacks on its buses, decided to honour the neighbouring strike by turning its long-distance buses back at the West Bromwich border. After two weeks the Corporation, anxious about the amount of media attention it was attracting, reversed its policy and ordered the buses to cross the border, but the Birmingham drivers refused. They even barred a BBC television crew from filming inside one of Birmingham's multi-racial bus depots because some of the men alleged that the programme would attempt to 'glorify' coloured workers.

After three weeks the strike folded and Patel, who had doggedly continued to work throughout, was officially accepted as a bus conductor. That was not the end of the battle, however. He continued to be ostracised by the majority of his fellow workers and individual conductors refused to take him on as a trainee. A year after the strike one of Patel's supervisors said of him: 'He's a nice quiet chap but he doesn't easily mix.'[20]

Elsewhere, black people were criticised for taking jobs away from whites and for undermining wages. One white youth said that he hated black people because 'I worked in a factory that wouldn't employ a white man, only a black man because he'll work cheaper – I got the sack through it. In my opinion they should be thrown out, the whole lot of them.'[21] But what seems to have bothered whites most about working alongside blacks was having to share amenities. They disliked having to sit on the same benches, drink out of the same cups, or use the same lavatories. Some factories even provided separate latrines for whites and blacks as they did in the southern States of America and South Africa.[22]

Shortly after black women began working in Nottingham's garment industry, employers noticed that the number of requests for transfers mysteriously began to rise. White women working in the same rooms as the new black employees asked to be moved to different sections. The management responded by segregating the staff. One of the senior managers in a textile factory which had taken this course by August 1956 explained how the new system operated: 'Our coloured girls now work on cheap goods under one white supervisor in their own department. Ultimately we hope to replace her with a coloured supervisor, preferably a girl with a keen sense of discipline.'[23] Black women were paid £3 to £4 a week, ostensibly because they were working on the cheapest clothes, while white women earned up to three times that amount. The branch official of the National Union of Manufacturers supported segregation, arguing that it was what most white workers wanted and that, in any case, black women liked to be together. The union claimed that, far from creating racial tension, it would satisfy both sides, as well as pleasing the management, which wanted harmony among its workers.[24]

Similar displays of opposition from white workers occurred in bus and rail depots across the country. In September 1955 white bus workers in Wolverhampton imposed a three-week overtime ban in protest against the employment of black platform staff. The local Transport and General Workers Union branch secretary denied that they were operating a colour bar. 'The men have made friends with the coloured men on the job, but we don't intend to have the platform staff made up to its full strength by coloured people only.'[25] Out of 900 employees in Wolverhampton's transport system, only 68 were black and the workers wanted that number reduced to the arbitrary figure of 52.[26]

The TUC and most executives of the national unions said they opposed racial strikes and colour bars of any sort. Occasionally, this brought them into direct conflict with their own local branches. In 1958 the National Musicians Union directed its Wolverhampton branch to boycott the Scala ballroom in protest against the dance hall's colour bar. The local branch refused, however, and its members continued to play there. As a result, the leaders of the Scala's three jazz bands were expelled from the national union, only to be re-admitted by the local branch, then expelled again. The struggle between the local and national level of the union was only resolved in February 1959 when the Scala changed ownership and the colour bar was dropped.[27]

Though the Musicians Union took a principled stance, most national unions hardly got beyond rhetoric. Even those unions which forged radical policies on Britain's external relations with her black colonies adopted a *laissez-faire* approach to the treatment of blacks at home. It was generally understood that day-to-day union affairs would be left to branch officials and that national union officers would only intervene locally over the most urgent matters. The colour bar was not generally considered one of those.

Meanwhile, at the local level some officials adopted traditional trade union terminology to rationalise their active opposition to the employment of West Indians. Black people, they said, were a threat to the English working class because they 'diluted' skills, sided with employers by breaking strikes and undermined the unions by refusing to join them. Unions zealously defended skills and specialisms as a main source of their bargaining strength. The beauty of skills, from the trade union point of view, is that they protect union members by making their work inexpendable. It follows that if skills are de-valued workers become more vulnerable. The determination of the unions to uphold skills and to restrict the entry of new workers into skilled trades was therefore understandable, but it had unfortunate consequences for the West Indians. The closed shop which was favoured by craft unions such as the printworkers, acted as an indirect colour bar. No black workers would be seen among the ranks of printers because union membership cards would only be issued to family and friends of existing white members.

In some instances West Indians were accused of watering down, or 'diluting' skills by taking work for which they were not properly qualified. This argument would have been justified had it not rested on the assumption that West Indian standards were lower than British. Many highly qualified West Indians were told that their qualifications were not acceptable and they were offered the choice of training all over again or giving up their trades. Harold Spencer spent five years as an apprentice tailor in Jamaica, but when he went looking for work in Nottingham he was told by both employers and the unions that this did not equip him to work in Britain where standards were more rigorous. What hurt most, he says, is that nobody would allow him to prove his abilities. Spencer has never worked as a tailor since coming to Britain in the 1950s.[28]

The second accusation made by the unions was that blacks were used by employers to break strikes. The term 'black-leg' was coined in 1865 and it was still being applied to strike breakers in the 1950s. In Liverpool, trade unionists claimed that West Indians were being taken on by employers in a conscious effort to accumulate a pool of strike-breakers. This was later shown to be pure fabrication.[29]

The third accusation was that black people undermined the unions by refusing to participate. Certainly, many black workers failed to join a union. In some cases this may have been due to indifference or apathy, in others to ignorance about the role and importance of unions. But the majority of black people did not join because they were not invited and because the unions appeared to them to be unhelpful or even openly hostile. In 1958 the TUC claimed that 'Here in Britain immigrants from many countries have been freely accepted into membership of trade unions and into industrial life.'[30] But this was not how Frances Ezzrecco, who is of Polynesian descent but who has lived all her life in London, saw it from ground level: 'Quite a number of so-called "brothers" didn't want black people in their unions. So all this talk about "brother" this and "brother" that at their meetings was a load of old nonsense.'[31]

In some industries, unions and employers joined forces in negotiating a 'colour quota', usually 10 per cent of the workforce.[32] Once the number of black workers had reached this level both sides would be armed with a set of stock arguments which they could produce on cue, like a well-rehearsed script:

Employer: Get a union card and I'll give you a job.
Union: Get a job and we'll give you a card.[33]

The unions were hoist by their own petard. By alienating potential black members they merely encouraged the formation of that which they feared most – a pool of non-unionised and disorganised labour which employers could potentially use to undermine the bargaining strength of the unions. Instead of making a concerted effort to encourage black people to join them, the unions lambasted West Indians for staying away. The General Secretary of the Transport and General Workers Union, Arthur Deakin, claimed that the strike in West Bromwich was a legitimate action taken against the threat of non-unionised labour: Patel was not a member of the TGWU so he had no right to work. He added that as far as he was concerned the strike was not racially motivated. 'It is the fear of unemployment that is behind this, and regard for experiences of the past. I do not for one moment accept the idea that there is any racial discrimination in this country.'[34]

As Deakin's statement indicates, much of the hostility of white workers and trade unionists stemmed from fears that the insecurity of the 1930s would one day return. In their battle against the spectre of the Depression, the unions relied on the closed shop and restrictive membership regulations to uphold precarious pay and working conditions. This hostility towards outsiders affected all workers struggling to enter trades. In 1948 the National Union of Mineworkers, for example, opposed the placing of more than three black miners per colliery.[35] But earlier, the NUM had drawn up similar, if less draconian, restrictions for the employment of Italian and Polish workers.

What distinguished the employment experience of black people from whites was that the former suffered twice over – once for being outsiders and again for being black. Many trade unionists were frightened by the prospect of blacks working among them. The unions in Birmingham, for instance, put up a bitter fight against black people working on the buses in the early 1950s. But as soon as the colour bar was dropped, black and white workers began to mingle and communicate and before long several depots were organising multi-racial football teams and cricket elevens. One union official admitted in 1954 that he was suprised how 'our people have adopted these coloured chaps. Before the coloured staff started work I thought the whole thing was a big mistake. I thought they would not be able to do the job. I have been proved wrong.'[36]

The combination of opposition from employers and unions hemmed the West Indians into the most menial and impecunious tasks. They were consistently down-graded and de-skilled. Of the West Indians who came in the 1950s, only 22 per cent had worked in the Caribbean in unskilled or semi-skilled jobs, yet once they arrived in Britain that figure rose to 63 per cent. Conversely, 24 per cent of the men and 50 per cent of the women left skilled or professional jobs behind in the West

Indies. But only 6 per cent of the men and 23 per cent of the women succeeded in finding equivalent work in Britain.[37] Pansy Jeffrey, for instance, was a trained health educator but she became so demoralised by the constant stream of rejections that she gave up applying for jobs in that profession and took up nursing instead.[38] Ruth Glass estimated that over one half of the West Indians experienced a similar fall in their status and economic position. The most extreme cases were middle-class professional people who found themselves suddenly relegated to the ranks of unskilled manual labourers. Indeed, Glass found that nearly 90 per cent of West Indian professional and skilled workers could only find manual work in London.[39]

The West Indians reacted in a variety of ways to their experiences in the workplace. Some swallowed their pride, accepted their lot and put on a smiling face whenever they experienced harassment or provocation from white colleagues. Others grew angry. Samuel Roberts, a Jamaican who has lived in Nottingham since the 1950s, was incensed by white workers who would trump up charges against him. He was constantly being pulled up in front of management for misdemeanours that he had not committed because his white co-workers wanted to see him fired. At times he would flare up and fight, but he soon learnt the pointlessness of violent protest which would only bar him from other factories. Instead, he packed his bags and quit. Roberts has had as many jobs in Britain as years he has spent here.[40]

That black workers were violent and sullen was a common complaint on the part of employers. When a group of West Indians approached their superintendent in the Royal Ordinance factory in Fazakerley, Liverpool, complaining of hostility from white co-workers, he said 'I have no hesitation in my conviction that they are unduly sensitive as regards remarks which may have been addressed to them.'[41] The trouble that this caused among existing workers was said to be one of the reasons why many employers, including the 'most broadminded', were reluctant to use black labour to relieve even the most persistent labour shortages.[42]

When West Indians reacted violently it was often because they had no other outlet for their grievances. They could not rely on the support of the trade unions in a dispute with management or fellow workers and they had no organised voice of their own. If they resigned this would reinforce the impression that blacks made unreliable employees. If they protested they would be blacklisted. And if they decided to grin and bear it, the abuse went unchecked.

Four months after the arrival of the *Empire Windrush* the *Orbita* brought 180 more West Indians to Liverpool, and three months after that another 39 Jamaicans, 15 of them women, came on the *Reina del Pacifico*. In the summer of 1949 the *Georgic* carried 253 West Indians to Britain, 45 of them women.[43] Like most migrant groups the West Indians congregated in those parts of the country where labour was most scarce and jobs easiest to find. Small West Indian communities began to develop in England's manufacturing and industrial centres, surpassing in numbers the older black settlements in the ports of Bristol, Cardiff, Liverpool and Newcastle. New West Indian arrivals were attracted to Nottingham by the abundance of work in its booming textile industries. In 1958 Nottingham had the fourth largest Afro-Caribbean community in Britain – 4,000 compared with slightly more in Manchester, 27,000 in Birmingham and 40,000 in London.[44]

The Attlee Government appeared unruffled by the influx of West Indians and Ministers made no public comment on the matter. Indeed, there seemed no reason why they should. The West Indians came of their own free will, paid their own passage, found their own accommodation and jobs, and went about their business like anybody else.

In private, however, Ministers and top civil servants were frantically debating how to respond to the newcomers' arrival. One of the most vexed questions that troubled successive governments in the 1950s was the issue of employment and whether or not to import black workers. The two ministries at the centre of the debate were at loggerheads. The Colonial Office was most concerned about unemployment and potential unrest in the West Indies; the Ministry of Labour was worried about unrest and potential unemployment in Britain. The Ministry of Labour deliberated over the political effects in Britain; the Colonial Office over the impact on Britain's relations with her colonies.

It was becoming increasingly evident in the 1950s that the attitudes of the British Government in Westminster and the colonial governments abroad had begun to grow apart. One reason for this was that the benefits of maintaining an empire had begun to be outweighed by the costs. Financially, the Caribbean was in dire straits, entirely dependent as it was on Britain for trade. In 1955 Britain took 45 per cent of the total exports from the West Indies and provided 40 per cent of imports.[45] While the economic dependence of the Caribbean had proved extremely profitable for Britain's merchants and manufacturers in the past, the Government was beginning to wonder whether the region was about to become a dead weight around its neck.

The Caribbean economy remained almost completely undeveloped. The traditional crop, sugar, still accounted for over half of the total produce of the West Indies and 90 per cent of Barbados' exports.[46] This emphasis on one crop put the economy at considerable risk. The West Indies produced only 3 per cent of world sugar supplies, so they were not in a position to dictate prices. When the predictable happened, and the bottom fell out of the sugar market in the late 1940s, inflation and unemployment rocketed, especially among the young.[47] Ironically, Britain, having begun her colonisation of the West Indies by forcing black people to work as slaves, ended it leaving thousands of West Indians without any work at all. Earlier attempts to diversify the Caribbean economy had had only limited success. Before 1914 the British encouraged the cultivation of coconuts and bananas in Jamaica and cocoa in Trinidad. But the new crops were plagued by disease, falling prices and a disastrous hurricane in 1944. Secondary industries remained at an embryonic stage of development. Trinidad and Barbados had small oil reserves, Jamaica a nascent textiles industry, and British Guiana a bauxite mine owned by the United States. But large-scale economic development was held back by the lack of infrastructure. Roads and rail links were primitive and haphazard and power and water supplies insufficient. New developments were frequently frustrated by the inherent inertia of the traditional plantation system. Three-quarters of the land in the British Caribbean was concentrated in one sixth of the total number of farms. These enormous plantations were not only grossly inefficient, they were also extremely resistant to change.[48]

In the 1950s Britain attempted to prop up the Caribbean economy by pledging to buy a fixed quantity of West Indian sugar at a guaranteed price. This was clearly intended as a temporary measure, especially as Britain could buy more cheaply from Cuba. To make matters worse, the population of the Caribbean islands was growing rapidly. Barbados, for instance, already had a population density of over 1,000 people per square mile – one of the highest in the world. If economic and demographic pressures were to continue unabated the West Indies could witness civil unrest on a scale unseen since the Jamaican strikes of 1938. By the early 1950s, alarming reports had begun to filter through to Britain. In Jamaica, Norman Manley's People's National Party was increasing its demands for higher wages and political independence, as was 'Busta' Bustamante's Jamaican Labour Party.[49] Then, in 1953, the People's Progressive Party (PPP) was elected in British Guiana on a socialist ticket. Westminster claimed the Party's leader, Dr Jagan, was aligned with 'international communism' and the Queen promptly suspended the new government. The dissolution of the PPP administration was greeted by mass demonstrations and strikes, which heightened the already charged political atmosphere throughout the Caribbean.

By the early 1950s the Colonial Office had begun experimenting with a number of different solutions to the West Indian crisis. Birth control programmes were launched, though these appeared to make little impact, and trading links were established between the West Indies and Europe in an attempt to reduce dependence on Britain. The most significant project was the Colonial Development Corporation, founded in 1948. This was a government-sponsored body set up to develop the use of natural resources through capital investment. The Corporation's fund of £30 million to invest over ten years was held up as evidence of Britain's commitment to the development of her colonies. However, it was too little, too late. Most of the money was put into primary products such as sugar and rice, rather than into manufacturing. Its impact on the material conditions of the mass of West Indian people was minimal. Per capita investment in the Caribbean remained one tenth the level in

Britain and in any case the money was treated as a loan rather than aid – the islands had to pay interest on it and eventually repay in full.[50]

The British Government desperately wanted to avoid the West Indies becoming a permanent drain on its resources.[51] Consequently, the proposals for tackling the West Indies' economic crisis which appealed most were those which cost least. One particularly draconian plan was to shift whole communities from one colony to another. It was suggested that 100,000 'surplus'[52] West Indians should be transported from the islands and settled in mainland British Honduras and British Guiana over a space of ten years.

The other solution which would not have required major capital investment was migration from the West Indies to Britain. The financial benefits were evident – it would cost only £100 to ship over West Indians to work in Britain's labour-starved industries, compared to the £4,000 it would cost to create one new job in the West Indies.[53] Moreover, the money that West Indian immigrants in Britain sent home to their families would act as a surrogate form of aid. Between 1950 and 1960, they sent £16.5 million to Jamaica alone, whereas the entire budget of the British Government's welfare programme for the West Indies in the 1950s amounted to only £15.5 million.[54]

The possibility of importing West Indians began to be seriously discussed by the British Government from 1948, at the time of the arrival of the *Empire Windrush*. A Colonial Office working party was set up to consider recruiting in the West Indies for British industries. It recommended that an experimental group of West Indians should be brought over to work in agriculture and textiles. They should preferably be women or married men to avoid 'social problems'.[55]

But Ministry of Labour officials were not convinced, arguing that employers would refuse to collaborate. They pointed to the National Institute of Houseworkers which said in 1949 that it would resist the entry of black people 'in view of the fact that the status of the domestic worker in this country might be prejudiced.'[56] The Board of Trade that governed the textile industry opposed the recruitment of Jamaican women, despite a shortage of 43,000 workers, because it said they would be illiterate and unlikely to stand up to the Lancashire climate.

The London County Council, forerunner of the GLC, refused to employ Bermudan women in its hospitals.[57]

The Ministry also had its own reasons for opposing the importation of West Indians. Apparently, black people could not work outdoors due to their susceptibility to colds and the more serious chest and lung ailments. Black women were reported to be slow mentally and to find considerable difficulty in adapting themselves to working conditions in this country. Only occasionally were the abilities and decorum of the West Indians openly, if somewhat patronisingly, recognised. 'From time to time,' wrote a Labour Department official in 1946, 'reference is made to the bad behaviour of coloured people. But I do wish to record that our West Indian scheme men should not be erroneously confused with other coloured people. It is thought that their association with the welfare section of the Department has taught them how to behave.'[58]

There was another important reason why the Ministry of Labour was not enthusiastic about importing black workers in the early 1950s – the immigration laws. Until 1948 West Indians, although technically British subjects, were restricted in their entry to Britain. This anomaly was removed in the Nationality Act of that year which gave all British subjects of the Commonwealth and Colonies the free and unrestricted right to live and work in Britain. The significance of this Act was swiftly appreciated by Ministry officials. It meant that they now had no direct control over the movement and employment of black workers from the colonies. They could come and go as they liked, work as much or as little as they desired, or even chose not to work at all in which case they were entitled to claim National Assistance.

In contrast, continental workers were much more acceptable. In addition to being white they were foreigners and so had none of the rights enjoyed by British West Indians. Classified 'aliens', they could be directed to the priority industries and if they left a job without permission, or 'misbehaved', they could be deported to one of the post-war camps for displaced persons on the continent. So stringent were these regulations that the British Government was censured in 1948 by the General Assembly of the United Nations, on the grounds that the European workers were 'victims of an official policy of discrimination'.[59]

Faced with the choice of either importing more Europeans or West Indians, the Ministry of Labour opted for the former. An official wrote in July 1948: 'It is one thing to maintain the traditional policy under which British subjects are free to enter Great Britain without restriction, but it is quite another thing to organise migration from one part of the Empire to another.' He added: 'the 500 men from the *Empire Windrush* have caused considerable political embarrassment by their mass arrival. It seems that no one wants the scheme. I suggest that we should welcome the opportunity of letting it die.'[60]

And let it die they did. Between the end of the war and 1950 around 100,000 Polish refugees and another 85,000 Italians and Eastern Europeans were recruited for British industries.[61] In October 1948 the Government even decided to bring over 6,000 German women to work in the textile factories.[62] The West Indians, who had served in the armed forces, were regarded as more of a liability than nationals of countries with which Britain had so recently been at war.

In 1948 the Government could afford to reject the idea of bringing black workers into Britain. The economy had only just begun to pick up after the war and although there was a need for extra labour it could be satisfied by Europeans. But by 1951 the British and Continental economies were relatively buoyant again and the European supply of workers had run dry. Production was expanding at a rapid 8 per cent per annum and exports soared, creating an even greater demand for labour. The King's speech on the opening of Parliament that year said 'My Government views with concern the serious shortage of labour, particularly skilled labour, which has handicapped production in a number of industries.'[63]

Fortunately for Britain, some West Indians continued to make their own way across the Atlantic, scraping together the boat fare or borrowing it from friends and relatives. The number of new arrivals each year rose and fell in direct proportion to the demand for labour in Britain.[64] In 1954 it was 24,000, climbing to 26,000 the following year but tailing off to 22,000 in 1957 and 16,000 in 1958. In the ten years between the arrival of the *Empire Windrush* and 1958 a total of 125,000 West Indians came to Britain.[65]

By the mid 1950s, however, the labour shortage had become so extreme that it surpassed the number of workers who had immigrated of their own accord. Machinery was lying idle and services were cut because of the lack of staff, especially in the least desirable, worst-paid jobs. The Government and employers had no choice but to abandon their earlier objections and begin recruiting black workers. In 1956, the British Transport Commission and London Transport sent officials to Barbados to seek new workers. A scheme was organised between the Barbadian colonial government and Westminster whereby individuals were lent 400 West Indian dollars to assist their passage. Four thousand black people came to Britain under this scheme, 40 per cent of whom went to work for London Transport. By 1958 there were over 8,000 black people working on London's buses and tubes. Hospitals signed up women in the West Indies for nursing and cleaning work and the British Hotels and Restaurants Association recruited Barbadians to work as chambermaids, porters and kitchen workers.[66]

But then the demand waned. The Suez crisis had led to oil shortages, pushing Britain into a minor economic recession. The Conservative Government aggravated the situation by squeezing credit in an attempt to cut inflation which brought unemployment back for the first time in a decade. By 1958 half a million people were jobless – a little over 2 per cent of the workforce.[67] As employers such as London Transport began to cut jobs and close garages, workers began to turn against the West Indians. The old complaints that black people were taking their jobs, lowering wages, and diluting skills began to be heard with increasing frequency. White men threatened to withdraw their wives from the buses, saying they did not know what to think when their wives worked late with black men. 'We are much more selective now,' said a recruiting officer, 'although there was a time when we were glad to take anybody. We used to be called Jamaica Inn. But not now.'[68]

Employers and trade unions in industries up and down the country contrived to soften the blow for white workers by ensuring that black people were the first to be made redundant. In Nottingham, for instance, over 13 per cent of West Indians were unemployed in 1958, although they formed only 1 per cent of the city's population.[69] 'Whenever I have to put off staff,' one employer admitted, 'I sack the coloured ones first. The trouble is that whenever you dismiss West Indians they make such a fuss. They say you have done it because of colour prejudice, and that makes you feel a rotter. But there would be a riot if I did anything else.'[70]

3

No Coloureds,
No Irish,
No Dogs

When Baron Baker was demobilised from the RAF he equipped himself with a smart suit and trilby and travelled south, arriving at Paddington in west London. This was a run-down area in the 1950s, full of seedy hotels and tawdry bedsits. For somebody with limited means it seemed as good a place as any to look for a room. But wherever he went Baker got the same reply – 'no rooms to rent'. Often landlords were more direct: 'No rooms for coloureds to rent'. Shop notices advertising bedsits read: 'No coloureds, no dogs, Irish not required'.[1]

'They didn't mind us fighting for them but when it came to living with them under one roof the iron gates slammed shut.' Some landlords banged the door in Baker's face. Others would say politely 'Oh! I'm so sorry, my wife has just let the place. I hope you have better luck elsewhere.'[2]

Discrimination of the sort that Baron Baker experienced in Paddington was widespread and entirely open. In 1958 a survey of a local paper in Notting Hill found that one in every eight of the 'To let' advertisements had 'No coloured' tags.[3] That didn't mean that the remaining seven welcomed West Indians, as Frances Ezzrecco discovered. Even though she had lived in England all her life she was treated as an outsider. She made a point of never revealing her colour over the phone. She would be offered a room, but when she arrived on the doorstep she would invariably be told that the room had gone. On one occasion a woman opened the door, looked at her and said 'Oh! you're coloured.' Ezzrecco took out a mirror from her handbag and replied: 'No, I'm not coloured, I'm brown all over. My eyes are brown, my hair is brown. *You* are coloured. Your eyes are blue, your skin is pink, and your hair is blond.' And she walked away.[4]

Frances Ezzrecco found it even harder to find accommodation after she married a West Indian jazz singer, Don, whose complexion ias darker than her own. Landlords would either send them both packing or offer only Frances a single room.

For the West Indians, the search for accommodation sometimes had a humiliatingly surreal quality. One landlady fainted on her doorstep when she saw her new lodgers.[5] In areas like Pimlico landlords had a reputation for throwing buckets of water over the heads of unsuspecting house hunters.[6] Trinidadian Chris Lemaitre used to spend every day in an estate agents in the West End, waiting for an offer of a bedsit. Every day he was told that they would soon find him a home, but they never did. English people would come into the agency and get a room immediately, at half the rent they were quoting him.[7]

A survey conducted in 1956 found that 90 per cent of landlords in London would not accept black student lodgers. Landlords gave varying reasons for rejecting blacks, from the vitriolically prejudiced, to the gently apologetic.

An example of the latter was a woman who thought black lodgers 'wouldn't fit in' and who was worried that she would not be able to satisfy their tastes: 'I like plain English fare,' she said, 'so I wouldn't be much good at cooking fancy foods.' More forthright was a middle-aged landlord with avowed left-wing sympathies, who said he was strongly opposed to all forms of prejudice but went on to describe how he had turned away a black lodger recommended by a political colleague. 'Nice sort of commie you are,' said his colleague. 'Won't even take a coloured comrade.' 'That's all very well,' retorted the landlord, 'but the darky would have been alone in the house. What if he gave boozing-parties and dragged girls off the street all night?' Asked for her opinions, a landlady said: 'I am not prejudiced. Only Jews, I don't like them. And blacks, of course, I don't like blacks. I am sorry for the darkies, that I am, but I know what my neighbours would say: "Look at her, she really has come down in the world." '

The objections raised by many landlords stemmed from their dread of the unknown, and it often transpired that those land-lords who did take black lodgers were pleasantly surprised by how little black people corresponded to their fearsome expec-tations. A young woman with two children, who had at first rejected black tenants because she thought them dirty, found living with them an educational experience. 'I am glad we took them. They are very nice, much more English than I had expected.'[8]

What most infuriated West Indians was that landlords would rarely accept responsibility for their actions. They did not object personally to blacks, they would say, but their other lodgers or neighbours might. As A.G. Bennett put it in 1954: 'What is wrong is with what they style the "neighbour" . . . Since I came here I never met a single English person who had any colour prejudice. Once, I walked the whole length of a street looking for a room, and everyone told me that he or she had no prejudice against coloured people. It was the neighbour who was stupid. If we could only find the "neighbour" we could solve the entire problem.'[9]

It was not only the poorest black people who suffered discrimi-nation. West Indians wealthy enough to rent in expensive areas had even less chance of finding a room than those looking for a bedsit in Paddington. One survey found that only 9 out of 111 landlords in Bloomsbury would rent to black lodgers.[10] Even black people who could afford to buy their own homes had to cope with unfriendly estate agents and solicitors. Houses were taken off the market for black house-buyers by having a colour bar written into their leases. The leaseholders were concerned that if their property was sold to black people it would lose capital value, so they simply inserted a clause preventing it from being sold to 'non-whites'.[11]

Hotels, from the seediest to the most glamorous in London, were also barred to black people. In 1953 an English firm of exporters and freight contractors tried to find accommodation in London for a party of visiting black businessmen. Fifty hotels and boarding houses turned them down. The businessmen were so offended they took their orders to the US.[12] Five years later, shortly before the Notting Hill riots, three well-to-do black women were given a cold reception by the manager of London's prestigious Goring Hotel. Despite having made reservations, they were told that some mistake must have been made – the rooms were all full. This provoked comment in the House of Commons. When the Attorney-General, Sir Reginald Manningham-Buller, was asked what action he would take against this colour bar, he replied 'None'.[13]

Even the Victoria League student hostel in Bayswater, west London – a body set up specifically to promote friendship between peoples of the Commonwealth – operated a colour bar. In 1957, one of the League's dignatories, Lord Altrincham, resigned in protest against its policy of only offering accommodation to white women and men. By his resignation he forced a limited change in policy. From being a mixed-sex all white institution it became a mixed-race women-only establishment. As Altrincham pointed out in disgust the new regime stemmed from the fear of mixing black men with white women: 'This is based upon the same odious and fantastic theory that inspired the previous policy of discrimination – that men and women who are differentiated only by the colour of their skins cannot be trusted to sleep under the same roof.'[14]

With nowhere else to go, the first West Indians to arrive in London after the war were literally forced onto the streets. Baron Baker ended up sleeping in charitable hostels for the homeless. More than once he had to spend the night in the Lyons Corner House, Piccadilly – a large entertainment centre with numerous restaurants and a dance floor that stayed open most of the night.[15]

At times it seemed as though there was no hope of ever getting a place to live. Council house waiting lists were either full or they required proof of five years residence in the locality, which the newcomers could not provide. There were few voluntary agencies to turn to for advice and assistance, and the West Indians could not expect much help from government welfare services. Some, like Donald Hinds, became so disillusioned they even suspected that the police would choose to ignore them if they tried, as a last ditch attempt to get a roof over their heads, to get arrested: 'In those days the police didn't even bother to pick up a black man, because the jail would be a night's shelter out of the rain and the cold.'[16]

*   *   *

Arriving in the Mother Country and discovering that your only home was the street would have been enough to turn anyone to drink – but even that proved problematic. Many pubs were out of bounds to black people, and others would only serve them in the public bar, the lounge being considered above their station. George Powe remembers battling against colour bars in Nottingham's pubs. The first he tackled was the 'Admiral Dundas', where the landlord refused to serve him under the pretext that single black men were not permitted. So he returned with a group of white friends and this time he was turned away on the grounds that they didn't serve black men in the company of white women.

Next he ventured into the 'Acorn' with a West African friend. Again they were refused a drink, so instead the two men went behind the bar and served themselves. When Powe asked the incensed landlord why he objected to black customers, he replied: 'Because you all bring prostitutes into the pub and I don't want that.' In a third pub, the 'Mechanics', the landlord threatened to unleash his large Alsatian on Powe. Undeterred, Powe returned with a large group of black and white friends who sat in the pub and refused to move until the police arrived.[17]

Many dance halls were also closed to West Indians. In August 1958, a few weeks before the riots broke out, the chain of Mecca halls was exposed in the press for operating its own peculiar form of colour bar in Nottingham, Birmingham and Sheffield. The policy was that only those black men who brought their own partners, whether black or white, would be allowed in and they were not allowed to 'pick up' another woman after entering. Mecca's Chairman, C.L. Heimann, insisted that he had no particular objections to black people and hotly denied that these restrictions constituted a colour bar. He said he would take similar precautions, if necessary, with Irish, Scots or Jews. It was merely a question of mixing oil with water. 'Man from the beginning of time has always been suspicious of strangers.'[18]

A few months earlier, in June 1958, the Scala luxury ballroom in Wolverhampton hit the headlines when an Indian engineering student, Udit Kumar das Gupta, invited his landlady to join him for a dance. He was refused entry by the thirty-year-old manager, Michael Wade. It was what his white customers wanted, he said. According to Wade, when blacks first started frequenting the dance hall he conducted an *ad-hoc* opinion poll, asking whites whether or not they wished to 'Let them in or keep them out?' 'The answer was so overwhelming I ordered that no coloured person was to be admitted. I feel strongly about personal freedom. Lots of people tell me they want to dance, but not with coloured people. I do not see why they should be forced to mix, and so long as I am here the ban will operate.' Underneath Wade's concern for personal freedom lay more sinister thoughts. 'Inter-racial marriages start in the ballroom – not in the factory,' he said.[19]

Although the Scala incident was covered by the media, it was not taken terribly seriously. At the height of the dispute, a local magistrate dismissed allegations of malpractice and renewed the dance hall's licence for another year. The local mayor said that he had no wish to shirk the issue, but he was not prepared to enter into this particular controversy. And a BBC *Panorama* team decided to drop plans to make a documentary on the Scala because their researchers uncovered colour bars in 29 other dance halls in the area, so they 'did not feel the Scala was unique'.[20]

But not everyone kept silent. The National Musicians Union made a principled stand and directed its members to boycott the Scala. As a result the union was hauled in front of the courts and disowned by its own local branch.[21] A local councillor, Harry Bagley, also spoke out against the colour bar. His reward was a pile of offensive letters, one of which contained a rope to hang himself. 'I used it to tie up my peas,' he said.[22]

Colour bars were allowed to flourish during the 1950s with remarkably little public comment or opposition. Successive governments either avoided discussing the issue or positively argued against the need for any action to curb discrimination. During the war, the only suggestion Ministers made to protect black RAF personnel from the harassment of white GIs was that the West Indians should be given little Union Jacks to pin on their lapels to distinguish them from black Americans, in the hope that if GIs did go 'nigger bashing' they would at least pick on their own countrymen.[23]

The law made no reference to racial discrimination. The established legal view held by government and the judiciary was that the law must be impartial, and should not distinguish between classes or types of people, including racial groups. The problem with this 'colour blind' approach was that it left no legal grounds for prosecuting those who practised racial discrimination. Landlords could refuse to house black people, dance hall owners could turn them away at the door, and employers could sack them, all entirely within the law. Although pub or hotel owners were legally prohibited from withholding entry to individuals whom they disliked personally, there was nothing to stop them from excluding entire racial groups because they disliked their common racial features. Black people had no positive redress: if they protested against a colour bar in a dance hall they were more likely to be arrested, for causing a disturbance, than the owner of the premises.

This happened to a Jamaican technician, George Roberts, during the war. Refused entry to the Liverpool 'Grafton' dance hall in 1943 due to pressure from American GIs, he stormed home, pulled on his Home Guard uniform and returned to the dance hall. Still barred, he swore his uniform had been insulted and announced that he would boycott the Home Guard until the colour bar had been lifted. He was subsequently arrested and fined £5 for failing to perform duties, although this ruling was overturned by a more sympathetic magistrate who reduced the fine to a nominal farthing.[24]

The Trinidadian cricketer, Learie Constantine, was the first person to challenge the colour bar in the courts. In the summer of 1943 he visited London to captain the West Indies against England at Lord's. But the hotel in which he was booked, the Imperial in Russell Square, refused to put him up for more than one night. 'We are not going to have all these niggers in our hotel,' they said. Constantine could not prosecute the hotel for discriminating against him on racial grounds, because no such offence existed. But he cleverly argued that although he had been turned away because he was black, this had caused him *personal* distress and injury. He won the case and was awarded token damages of £5. More important, he set a precedent in civil law against the colour bar.[25]

But Constantine's action, which received considerable publicity at the time, did not convince Westminster of the need for legislative change. Conservative Ministers in the 1950s, consistently opposed legislation against racial discrimination basing their resistence on three fallacious arguments. The first was that the best way of eradicating prejudice was by educating public opinion. However, the Government did not take any steps to introduce education programmes on race relations in schools or colleges and throughout the whole of the 1950s it made no public statement on the subject.

Second, it was argued that legislation would interfere with the individual liberties of landlords and employers. The state should not become involved in private disputes between employers and their workforce or landlords and their tenants. In 1957 the Government announced at an international conference on labour relations that it would not outlaw discrimination in the workplace as this would infringe the rights of employers to run their businesses as they wished.[26] The weakness of this argument, of course, was that the clear distinction between public and private domains had been blurred in the nineteenth century. It had been established then that government had the right to intervene in the private realm if this was in the public interest. The Factory Acts of 1874 and 1875 imposed regulations on how employers treated women and children. And in housing, rent controls in force since 1915 limited the personal freedom of landlords by restricting the rents they could charge their tenants.

The final argument was that legislation was not required to outlaw discrimination since none existed in the United Kingdom.[27] This claim, again, was disingenuous because it belied the fact that the Government was itself involved in discriminatory practices. Some employment exchanges (the equivalent of job centres in the 1950s) dealt with unemployed blacks separately from whites. In one exchange personal data cards were marked yellow for Irish people, green for people who had been in Britain for over 20 years, blue for less than 20 years.[28] In another, black people's files were marked 'coloured'. When a Jamaican who had recently served in the RAF discovered this he threw his serviceman's book at the clerk and shouted 'This isn't marked "Coloured"'! No one in the Air Force cared whether I was coloured or not, why should you?'[29]

The labour exchange in Stepney, east London, had a separate 'coloured section' with its own waiting room and staff. Officials argued this was to the benefit of the West Indians because the staff learnt how to understand their 'peculiarities'.[30] In an exchange in Camden Town, north London, half the total number of employers in the borough stipulated no blacks.[31] Most exchanges denied that they distinguished between blacks and whites, though some were more candid and admitted that they made special arrangements to 'spare' black people the trouble of applying for jobs which they would never get. A West Indian in Birmingham, skilled in metalwork and fluent in three languages, drew a blank whenever he went to the labour exchange. 'I am sorry for you,' he was told. 'It is talent wasted, but the factories will not employ coloured men. Do not blame us. Blame the management and they in turn will blame their employees. British workers do not like sharing their benches with a coloured man and that's an end of it.'[32]

One month after the arrival of the *Empire Windrush*, fighting broke out in a Ministry of Labour hostel at Castle Donington, Nottingham. Black residents were set upon by whites described as 'Irish and certain foreign elements'.[33] Although the manager of the hostel, W. Hardman, did not dispute the fact that white people had started the fight, he decided to evict the West Indians. 'It was unfortunate,' he said, 'that the practical needs of the situation made it necessary to remove the minority.'[34]

The following year a hostel in Causeway Green near Birmingham was virtually destroyed when a miniature race riot broke out. The hostel's sleeping quarters had been segregated into white and black areas, which some West Indians cited as one of the causes of the fighting. Armed with sticks, stones and razors, 200 Polish residents fiercely attacked the West Indian quarter, where 65 men were billeted. They said they were wreaking revenge on the black men, whom they accused of entertaining women in their cubicles night and day.[35] A sleeping West Indian was coshed over the head with a brick and nearly 400 windows in the huts were smashed before the police arrived. Witnesses said the fight was like a scene from a Hollywood gangster movie:

police whistles screeching, crowds of men running, young white girls screaming.[36]

The brawl was a source of great embarrassment for the Government. Local residents organised a petition calling for the removal of the 'coloured element' or the closure of the hostel. They had been particularly upset, they said, by West Indians climbing into their backyards to escape. Again, the authorities' preferred remedy was to remove the West Indians. The local police superintendent said 'I'm sorry about it, because 90 per cent of these coloured boys fought for the country in the armed forces. But it is easier to move 65 men than 200.'[37] Top government officials, having been dragged into the affair, suggested that four of the most 'undesirable' West Indians should be publicly expelled from the hostel as an exemplary punishment. Meanwhile, the police announced that they would not prosecute any of the white men for lack of evidence.[38]

But the West Indians refused to budge, staging a sit-down protest outside their huts. If they were forced to leave, they said, they would lose their jobs in local factories. And as the longest-standing residents they saw no reason why they should be punished for a fight which they did not initiate. Horace Halliburton spoke for all the West Indians when he said: 'We consider it very unfair that, though we are British, we are the people to suffer.'[39] In response, government officials hit on the more diplomatic plan of dispersing West Indians gradually until their numbers had been reduced to thirty.[40]

The Causeway Green incidents gave the government Hostels Corporation the green light to revive the call for a colour quota. West Indians, they said, were fine on their own but putting them together in a crowd was like setting a match to a haystack. 'However charming they may be individually, these West Indians do tend to get across, and then to start fighting with, other residents, in particular the Irish and the Poles.'[41] The Nottingham regional hostels controller said they were 'childish, insolent and arrogant and a large number of them are undoubtedly looking for trouble . . . They have the reputation of being good workers, but in the hostel and in the village they showed a childish pride in their British citizenship and arrogantly claimed all sorts of privileges on the basis of it.'[42]

Although the Labour Government resisted the Corporation's demands for a colour quota for over a year, it finally agreed to place a ceiling on the numbers of West Indian residents in every government hostel in the country. In 1950 officials from the Ministry of Labour and the directors of the Hostels Corporation met to fix quotas. The upper limit was set at 30 blacks, or 10 per cent of the total number of residents if less. Hostels regarded as potential trouble spots were given a lower limit of 12 black people, while some hostels barred West Indians altogether.[43] From March 1950, wardens were prohibited from taking more than their quota even if they did not personally object to black residents.

This colour bar remained government policy throughout the 1950s. In 1954, six years after the fighting in Causeway Green, the Government debated whether to drop the quota system, but concluded that it was still necessary: 'We would be unwise to tinker with this agreement. The press had not heard of the Mau Mau when we were having our racial fights in Birmingham and we dare not assume that the attitude to coloureds is so much improved since those days that we can take undue risks.'[44]

Yet the Labour Government that had initiated the colour bar, and successive Conservative administrations, consistently denied that any official discrimination existed. One reason why they tried to keep the hostels' colour quota secret was that it would have been highly unpopular with those employers who wanted black workers for their labour-starved industries. From 1954, employers were told by the Government that they could have no more West Indian workers because there was nowhere to house them. One irate employer had his request for extra West Indian workers turned down because the nearest government hostel had already reached its quota of 15 and no more could be accommodated, even though there were 100 empty beds.[45]

The only attempts to outlaw discrimination during the 1950s came from individual MPs in the form of Private Members' Bills. In 1951 a Labour politician, Reginald Sorensen, introduced the first Bill against colour bars in public places, followed a few months later by another Bill launched by Fenner Brockway. In the eleven years between 1953 and 1964 this Labour MP made a further nine attempts to persuade Parliament to legislate against discrimination.[46]

These parliamentary debates were poorly attended and many Members who did turn up seemed to regard the issue as a relatively light-hearted affair. One MP compared the West Indians' plight with that of dogs who, to the great consternation of their owners, were barred from lodging houses. Another said: 'We cannot compel people to love one another, any more than we can ignore the fact that some people talk more loudly, take fewer baths, wear dirtier clothes, or have more unpleasant habits, than others. Where racial prejudice does exist it calls for education, sympathy and knowledge, but it certainly does not call for legislation.'[47]. The Government repeated the same complacent arguments against the need for legislation as each Private Member's Bill was heard and dismissed. In 1954 Prime Minister Churchill was asked what measures he intended to introduce to combat the colour bar. 'The laws and customs of this country upon this subject are well known,' he replied. 'I am advised there is no need for new instructions.'[48] Only once did any of these Bills enjoy a second reading, on three Fridays early in 1957 for a total of sixty minutes, after which the Bill was counted out because fewer than the requisite forty Members had bothered to turn up.[49]

4

From Rachman to Ruin

The lack of official action against colour bars left the West Indians to fend for themselves. They had no alternative but to live wherever landlords would take them. In London, as in most cities where black people congregated, this left them with very little choice. They could rule out expensive and exclusive areas like South Kensington, Highgate and Westminster where even well-off black people would not be entertained. Staunch working-class districts with stable populations, south of the river and in parts of the East End, were equally hard to penetrate.[1]

The options open to the newcomers were further restricted by the housing crisis that gripped parts of England in the 1950s. Half a million properties had been destroyed by the war in Britain as a whole. In London, over 100,000 had been destroyed or so seriously damaged as to require rebuilding and a further million homes needed war damage repairs of some sort. At the same time, demand for housing had increased dramatically through demobilisation and the return of London's evacuees, together with a boom in marriages and births. By 1951 there were nearly 500,000 more households in London than homes.[2]

By then the housing shortage generally, and in London in particular, had become a top political priority. One of Churchill's manifesto commitments in the 1951 elections was to build 300,000 new houses annually, a popular gesture which helped to oust the Labour Government and throw Churchill back into the political driving seat. To its credit, the incoming Tory administration kept its promise. Harold Macmillan, whom Churchill appointed to lead the quest for more housing, surpassed the 300,000 homes mark within two years. Much of the new building was concentrated in London's outer ring, which helped to filter people out of congested inner London to the suburbs.[3]

But having achieved his target, Macmillan began siphoning resources from the public to the private sector. Local authorities were encouraged to put their money into private homes, rather than into council housing. By the end of the decade, the number of council houses built each year had fallen to half its 1953 peak, while the quantity of new private houses increased in the same period by a factor of five.[4]

Thousands of families became owner-occupiers for the first time, including skilled working-class people with steady jobs. But although the new suburban propertied class undoubtedly prospered with Macmillan at the helm, for those left behind in the inner cities the situation rapidly deteriorated. Rented accommodation was in short supply and public investment in old housing stock squeezed, which left bomb-damaged and dilapidated inner-city areas degenerating at an alarming rate.[5] Indeed, more slums were created during the fifties through disrepair and neglect, than were knocked down.[6] Sir Milner Holland, who conducted an investigation into London's housing, concluded that although the housing stock had improved overall, there were pockets in London which had deteriorated to 'conditions which were more akin to those prevailing in the nineteenth century'.[7]

The people who were affected most severely by Macmillan's housing policy were the most disadvantaged and vulnerable groups: elderly people, young single men and women, unskilled workers and the unemployed, people with low incomes, and newcomers. The disadvantaged, above all, were the West Indians who as young, predominantly single people lacking the capital to buy a house or even furniture, were looking for bed-sitting rooms to rent. Excluded from whole districts, they were trapped in the worst parts of the city. Learie Constantine, despite his pre-eminence in both sporting and political fields, spent most of his life in Britain living in poor accommodation.

'After practically 25 years residence in England,' he wrote in 1954, 'where I have made innumerable white friends, I still think it would be just to say that almost the entire population of Britain really expect the coloured man to live in an inferior area devoted to coloured people, and not to have free and open choice of a living-place. Under these conditions a coloured person is permitted to live in Britain. This is the "equality" shown between white and black citizens of the British Empire and Commonwealth.'[8]

Baron Baker eventually found a room of his own in west London, having spent a year relying on charity and friends. He used to drink in a pub in Notting Hill with black seamen friends, and through them he discovered the first landlady in the area prepared to take black tenants – Mrs Fisher in Tavistock Road. 'Her neighbours used to call her white-trash-nigger-lover because she associated with us. But she was liberal-minded and didn't care. Her rooms were all rented and she made plenty of money. She laughed at her neighbours because they weren't enjoying the life she was enjoying.'[9]

The West Indians made up for the shortage of housing open to them by supporting each other. Fresh arrivals would be offered a floor to sleep on by their friends or relatives until they had found somewhere of their own. King Dick came over from Jamaica in 1954 and, having spent three weeks in prison for stowing away, he occupied his first free day in England by wandering around Notting Hill. As he was strolling down Tavistock Road, Baron Baker stuck his head out of his bedroom window and asked him where he was going. They got talking and Baker told him where he could rent a room in the area. King Dick spent the next ten years living in west London and has remained Baker's close friend ever since.[10]

Notting Hill was an extremely disparate area. Bound by Holland Park Road to the south and the Harrow Road to the north, it encompassed strikingly different communities and embraced the extremes of wealth, with millionaires living a street away from the destitute. Notting Hill Gate proper was, as it still is, home to London's *élite*, counting among its residents ambassadors, judges and the wealthy. Just a few streets to the north of Notting Hill Gate, along Ladbroke Grove, is the Colville area. This consists of large five-storey houses built in the 1860s by property developers hoping to profit from the mid-nineteenth century expansion in London's population. However, their plans backfired and the houses in Colville never became middle-class family homes as intended. Instead, they were divided into tenements and filled with a succession of migrant groups beginning with the Irish.[11] In the 1920s it was known locally as 'Little India' because some of its houses were inhabited by Asians studying for the Indian Civil Service Exams.[12] Marcus Garvey lived here in the 1930s. By the 1950s the Colville area was home to a large Eastern European community, together with Irish people, Cypriots and Maltese.

It was into the Colville area that the West Indians moved, first into Mrs Fisher's house and then into the property of other landlords who began opening their doors to black people as soon as they realised the financial benefits. The newcomers were a windfall for landlords in Notting Hill because they could be charged extravagant rents, with often four people per room, paying per head. Baron Baker used to pay £4 a week rent out of his weekly earnings of £5.[13] West Indians were driven to hiding friends in their rooms to bring down the rents. If they got five people into a room which the landlord thought was only occupied by one, each would pay one fifth of the rent. Pansy Jeffrey lived in a miserable little room, with innumerable others. The landlord packed the house with Asians, West Africans and West Indians. Although this made the house rather cramped, it did have modest advantages. Every time Pansy Jeffrey asked whether one more person could stay in her room, the landlord would say 'OK my dear, if you pay another pound'.[14]

Black people were almost invariably confined to the worst part of the building, in damp basements, cupboard rooms, or even landings. Overcrowding was rampant – the Colville area had the highest degree of overcrowding outside Glasgow.[15] Whole families lived in single box-rooms, cooking on small gas stoves which they set up on the landings, with no hot water or baths and sharing one lavatory between fifty people. Three out of every four households had no hot water and 60 per cent had no baths.[16] Life was especially hard for West Indian women who started arriving in Britain in greater numbers from 1955. They tended to spend more time at home and were in charge of domestic finances and child care. Trying to look after children in those congested and insanitary conditions must have been extremely difficult, quite apart from stretching their meagre wages to the end of the week. West Indian women were forced to work long shifts on top of raising a family and often had to support dependent relatives back in the West Indies as well.[17]

Notting Hill was the centre of the empire of the notorious racketeering landlord, Peter Rachman. Rachman came to England from Poland during the war without a penny to his name; he died in 1962 a millionaire. This fortune was made through the cunning manipulation of his tenants and the rent laws. Until 1957 unfurnished accommodation was rigidly controlled and rents were frozen at affordable levels. He would buy these properties for around £3,000 through one of the many property companies he set up in other people's names to hide his traces. Using front men he would then negotiate five separate mortgages on different parts of the house, raising at least £10,000. Incoming rents would pay for the outgoing mortgage repayments, leaving him with a clear profit of £7,000.[18]

But raking in a few thousand pounds through mortgage fiddles was small fry to Rachman. He knew that while unfurnished rents were strictly controlled, the rents of furnished bedsits were almost entirely free of any legal restrictions. All Rachman had to do was persuade his sitting controlled tenants to leave, add a mouldy mattress and a rotten chair or two, call the new tenancy 'furnished' and charge the new tenants any amount he liked.[19]

The only protection for tenants of furnished bedsits were rent tribunals, which could set a fair rent if tenants applied in person. But this offered no real threat to Rachman. All he had to do was dissuade his tenants from approaching the tribunals, and he had a simple, but very effective, method for this – brute force. Hired henchmen made regular visits to Rachman's tenants to collect his exorbitant rents or to see to their eviction. Tenants who worked in the day would return to find all their belongings strewn across the street, rubbish emptied in the middle of the living room, itching powder sprinkled in their bedding or dead rats left under the sheets.[20] Rachman was even said to have hired builders to lift off the roof of one of his houses in order to remove some particularly stubborn tenants.[21]

He also had his own paramilitary force of bully boys who used to scour the area with vanloads of Alsatian dogs. 'They would beat you up as quick as look at you. If you didn't pay your rent on time there was no hope – you'd be in hospital the same day.'[22]

West Indians formed a large proportion of Rachman's tenants because they fitted perfectly into his scheme of things. They could be charged extortionate rents, as they had nowhere else to live; they could be forced into multi-occupation and charged per head; they even helped him to buy up new properties on the cheap because house prices in a street plummeted as soon as black people moved in. If he had trouble with recalcitrant white tenants Rachman would move black lodgers next door and where Alsatian dogs and bully boys had failed to drive tenants out, the shock of having black neighbours often succeeded. Rachman started buying houses in the centre of the Colville area of Notting Hill in 1955, in St Stephens Gardens, and his empire expanded almost in direct proportion to the growth of Notting Hill's West Indian community. By 1958 he owned around 100 houses in the West London area.[23]

George Clark, a community worker who was involved in the campaign to break Rachman's empire after the riots, used to visit West Indians in rooms which were divided by tape into six sections. In each section was a bed and in each bed was a sleeping West Indian. One could be sure that the bed was always occupied because there was a day shift and night shift.[24] Tenancies were granted on a weekly basis, and only a few hours notice of eviction would be given.

In 1957 the new Macmillan Government decided that housing legislation was weighted so much in favour of the tenant that it was preventing landlords earning an honest profit. Rent controls were so restrictive, they argued, that landlords were taking their money out of rented accommodation and investing it elsewhere. What was needed, therefore, was a freeing of controls to encourage landlords to keep their capital in rented housing. What followed was the 1957 Rent Act[25] which decontrolled the unfurnished sector. In London 135,000 tenancies were lost to the controlled sector overnight. All other tenancies were under 'creeping decontrol' which meant they lost their security as soon as they changed hands, which naturally encouraged Rachman to step up harassment to remove old tenants.

For tenants in Notting Hill rents more than doubled in twelve months and by 1958 over 200 notices of eviction were served in this area alone.[26] The Kensington Tenants' Association said that the legislation: 'allows much real evil, encourages oppression of the poor and offers tenants bogus rights, no security of tenure, makes enforcement of repair a farce, and will unless repealed surely lead to widespread civil disobedience'.[27]

The only body which could really have brought Rachman to heel was the local authority. But improving housing conditions in Notting Hill had never been one of the priorities of the Royal Borough of Kensington. It had one of the lowest levels of council housing in London,[28] and a very poor record on prosecuting landlords for the overcrowding or disrepair of their properties. The borough covered not only run-down North Kensington which included Notting Hill, but also wealthy Holland Park, Kensington proper and South Kensington, where most of the Conservative councillors, who were in the majority on the council, lived. The northern part of the borough was regarded with pity but no real interest, like a poor relative. Although the council had the power to take Rachman to court on behalf of his tenants not one case was brought to rent tribunal before the riots.[29] The council even refused to receive a deputation from a local tenants' association to discuss the housing crisis on the grounds that two of the association's members belonged to the Communist Party.[30] So Rachman ran his racket with impunity. By 1958 he was already an extremely wealthy man. He owned six cars including a Rolls Royce, and dressed in silk shirts with diamond cuff-links and hand-stitched crocodile-skin shoes. While his tenants lived in dirt and squalor, he owned a luxury house in Hampstead Garden Suburb and is said to have been so obsessed with cleanliness that he bathed three times a day in strong Dettol mixture.[31]

Rachman's subsequent notoriety gave rise to the expression 'Rachmanism', a catch-all term used to describe the practices of lawless profiteering landlords. But there was an ambivalence about Rachman which has been largely overlooked or forgotten. Despite his crooked ways, he was also one of the only landlords in London prepared to house black people. Of course, he did this for financial rather than altruistic motives, but from the

West Indians' point of view a box-room in one of Rachman's overcrowded and dilapidated houses was better than no room at all. 'At the time,' says Baron Baker, 'I didn't see Rachman as a rogue but as a saviour. Where else could you go? I don't feel he was a bad man even now.'[32] The ambivalent attitude of the black community towards Rachman was symbolised by Michael de Freitas who became one of Rachman's henchmen, in charge of a group of houses in the Colville area.[33] 'Michael was the sort of plausible front that Rachman used because it made you wonder if they really were hit men,' says David Mason, a Methodist minister based in Notting Hill from the late 1950s. 'He was so charming that you thought it was all exaggeration and hearsay.'[34] George Clark, who in 1959 organised tenants into an association in an attempt to break Rachman's hold, remembers being summoned to see de Freitas one Boxing Day. Over lunch de Freitas casually offered him four houses in Powis Terrace if he disbanded the association. Clark left abruptly, before the Christmas pudding.[35]

In his autobiography, Michael de Freitas explained why for him Rachman was not the malefactor in this story:

> The real villain was not Peter Rachman. It was, and still is, all those who put up notices saying: 'No coloured' ... 'No Irish' ... 'No children' ... 'No dogs' – 'No' people: nasty, mean, ignorant, joyless people. They're the ones who made it possible for Rachman to provide his particular kind of service. They and the well-meaning people who condemn him but do nothing about the situation that created him.[36]

In 1958, the Colville area of Notting Hill was bursting at the seams. The once elegant five-storey terraced houses were crumbling under the pressure of extreme overcrowding and neglect. By the 1980s the houses had been renovated and commanded prices of hundreds of thousands of pounds. But in the 1950s the plaster was falling away from the outside walls, exposing large patches of bare brick; the balconies were falling apart; and the windows were unpainted and rotten. All but the last traces of discoloured paintwork had pealed off the front doors. Occasionally there would be a gap in the line of houses, left by a fallen building.[37]

Notting Hill in the 1950s bears no comparison to the

gentrified area it was to become in the following decades. The air was thick with fumes from local factories and the streets covered in rubbish, derelict cars and broken milk bottles glistening like snow. In Talbot Grove there was an open rubbish dump in the middle of the street, three feet high with rotting vegetables and unrecognisable animal matter. On a cold day the stench was clearly distinguishable; on a hot day, abominable. Children could be found playing among piles of rubbish, which included dead cats and chickens crawling with maggots.[38] At night the streets were dark and it was a hazard simply negotiating one's way between the broken glass and rubbish.[39] Colin MacInnes wrote that the area was nothing more than a stagnating slum. 'It's dying this bit of London and that's the most important thing to remember about what goes on there. . . man, I tell you, you've only got to be there for a minute to know there's something radically *wrong*.'[40]

But the area had its compensations. West Indians had the comfort of being together. By 1958 Notting Hill was home to 7,000 West Indians and it was popularly called 'Brown Town' – a pun on nearby White City. Its population was extremely cosmopolitan, with over 60 per cent born outside the UK in 1961.[41] It had a youthful, unregimented atmosphere which West Indians explored to the full, congregating in the few pubs which would accept them. When Baron Baker first went to Notting Hill one of the places he frequented was the 'Apollo' pub in the All Saints Road. At first black people were only served in the public bar, not in the saloon, but as the owner began to realise that there was lucrative business to be made out of them he dropped the colour bar entirely. Once a pub had been 'liberalised', word spread like wild-fire and before long it would be packed with black people from all over London.[42]

Although the number of pubs where they could drink was limited, black people made up for it by organising their own late-night drinking and dancing sessions: 'Shebeens' as they were called, the fifties equivalent of latter-day Blues parties. An improvised, unlicensed bar would be set up in the corner of someone's front room and a record player would blast out the latest sounds – jazz, soul or calypso.

West Indian clubs and Shebeens started up all over the Colville area. A Barbadian called 'Bajay' opened a coffee house and music club in a basement in Talbot Road. Michael de Freitas, when he wasn't busy working for Rachman or running gaming houses, used to hold Shebeens with live music in a basement flat. Wilfrid Woodley, the jazz pianist, was a regular performer at these events.[43] But for the big-time music stars, both black and white, West Indians had to travel into central London, to one of the many jazz venues: to the 100 Club in Oxford Street where Humphrey Lyttleton was resident; or Club 11 in Carnaby Street which was home to the Johnny Dankworth Seven. Other popular late-night spots were the Sunset Club in Carnaby Street or the Paramount in Tottenham Court Road. Here black people could mingle freely with white women and men, on equal terms and without fear of trouble.[44]

For when it came to jazz music, people left their prejudices behind. It was one of the few professions where black people were recognised and excelled – like Trinidadian Winifred Atwell who came to Britain to learn classical piano but found that she could earn ten times as much playing honky tonk as sonatas. She sold over ten million records and appeared on television and in variety shows. There was Russ 'Jiver' Henderson and his big steel band and the older generation, veteran musicians like Leslie Hutchinson, the Jamaican trumpeter, and Yorke de Saya, a pianist from Trinidad who played at the 500 Club.[45] And, of course, the queen of them all, Lady Day, whose visits sent ripples of excitement through the jazz world and attracted huge crowds, black and white. Billie Holiday's haunting version of *Strange Fruit*, portraying the stark horror of the lynch-law of the American South, must have made the West Indians in London feel that things could have been worse.

> Scent of magnolia, sweet and fresh,
> Then the sudden smell of burnin' flesh

Back in Notting Hill most people would play guitar, fife or drums. If they didn't they would scrape on a cheese grater or bang on the tables, turning everyday objects into musical instruments. Baron Baker spent a lot of his time in Notting Hill playing dominoes, cards or ludo with friends at a café at 9 Blenheim Crescent. The 'Fortress', as it was affectionately known by those who frequented it, was owned by a Jamaican called Totobag. 'That was our meeting ground,' says Baker. 'People from all over would go there looking for friends. They always made contact in the end. The Fortress was like a centre for us, a home, it was our everything.'[46] Thrown together in a hostile world, West Indian men and women depended on this kind of mutual support and assistance. Totobag was like a father figure to many of the new arrivals, welcoming them and smoothing their entry into London life. 'He would even break up his furniture to put on the fire to keep his visitors warm – he was a very soulful man,' says an old friend who still remembers him vividly.[47]

The Fortress was primarily frequented by Jamaicans. Sixty per cent of the West Indians who came to Britain in the 1950s were from Jamaica[48] and until after the 1958 riots contact between nationals of different Caribbean islands was limited. For some West Indians the experience of mixing with people from different parts of the Caribbean was quite disturbing. So was the fact that middle-class and working-class black people were all thrown together. West Indians tended to define themselves in the 1950s more in terms of class than race. Thus middle-class West Indians expected to mix with English people from similar professional backgrounds. Likewise, working-class West Indians did not imagine that in England they would be rubbing noses with wealthy Jamaicans who back home they would normally only meet in the role of domestic servant. Suddenly, they were thrown into a melting pot and stirred. Sons and daughters of Jamaican notables lived underneath labourers from the shanty towns, in the same rotten houses. Jamaicans lived with Barbadians and Trinidadians with Dominicans.

Inevitably, black and white people also mixed in the Colville area of Notting Hill. With West Indians and young white families living in the same room separated by only a thin chipboard partition, they could hardly have done otherwise. One couple's Saturday night brawls belonged to the couple in the next room, as did their sexual idiosyncrasies.[49]

Baron Baker remembers that many of his white friends were older generation, middle-class liberals who had worked in the colonies on voluntary service. 'They had travelled the world, they knew us in our home setting and so they understood where we were coming from.'[50] The white people who mixed among the West Indians came from remarkably varied backgrounds, from men like 'Peanuts' – a thief who used to make sorties in

the heavy smog to raid jewellers shops[51] – to celebrities such
as Brian Jones of the Rolling Stones and David Hockney. The
writer Colin MacInnes was a regular visitor to Notting Hill,
attracted by its cosmopolitanism. MacInnes' fascination with
'Spades' began in 1952 when he became caught up in a social
whirl surrounding the tour of the black American Katherine
Dunham dance company. Subsequently he immersed himself
in London's growing West Indian and West African scene
in the café quarter of Cable Street in the East End, Soho
clubs and Notting Hill. These areas formed the backdrop
to the first two volumes of his London trilogy: *City of Spades*
(1957) and his classic account of the Notting Hill race riots
– *Absolute Beginners* (1959). 'MacInnes was one of the most
sympathetic characters working with us,' remembers Horace
Ove. 'I don't think there's ever been another white writer
who has exposed themselves to blacks as Colin did. He did
it at *every* level, from African chiefs to pimps and prostitutes
and down-and-outs.'[52] MacInnes impressed men like Horace
Ove because he treated them as he treated everyone else.
When he thought you were wrong he would tell you, or shout
at you. He was neither denigrating nor patronising. MacInnes
was drawn to Notting Hill by its combination of white and
black, rich and poor and by the vivacity and spontaneity of
the place. 'Napoli' he called it, and indeed it had a lot more in
common with Naples than with South Kensington only a mile
across Hyde Park.

While MacInnes and a few other white men welcomed, and
were welcomed by, the West Indian community in London,
most of the West Indians' English friends were women. Part of
the reason for this was undoubtedly sexual. In the early 1950s
there were few West Indian women coming to Britain. Until
1955, when the numbers began to even out, 85 per cent of the
West Indian newcomers were men, most of whom were single.[53]
Consequently, black men used to liaise with local white women,
and they often married.

But the sexual element was only one factor. Horace Ove says
that women were the only sympathetic people who reached out
to black men. 'It wasn't that white women fancied this "gigolo
out of the jungle" as people used to make out. They were curious,
and despite pressure from their parents and friends they helped

us by reaching out to us. They had understanding for us for some reason.'[54]

Perhaps one point of contact between white women and black men which might help explain Ove's feeling of communality between them is that, in their daily lives, they suffered from many of the same kinds of prejudices. Like West Indians, women had been indispensable during the war, but as soon as peace was signed they were told to get back to where they had come from, namely, the home. Women were also given the worst jobs and barred from promotion. Like the West Indians they were often regarded as stupid, incompetent and incapable of holding positions of responsibility. In short, both white women and black men were demeaned by white men.[55]

West Indian men mixed with women of all classes and backgrounds, from the very poor to the very rich. One woman who made a regular appearance on the West Indian scene was Sarah Churchill,[56] Winston's favourite child. 'She used to hang out with us,' says Baron Baker. He met her in the Sunset Club and King Dick spent many evenings with her at Totobag's. She would arrive in her Rolls Royce and, leaving her driver sitting outside, mingle with the crowd until closing time in the early hours. For her, as for Colin MacInnes, mixing with black men was a way out of her restrained social circle, an escape from high-society prudery.

A number of the women who lived in the Colville area and who mixed with West Indians worked as prostitutes. At that time England was experiencing a post-war moral backlash, aimed largely against two groups – prostitutes and homosexuals. Police activity had been stepped up against both groups, using plain-clothes officers to infiltrate their pubs and meeting places. In 1957 the Wolfenden Report recommended tough new laws on homosexuality and proposed that prostitution should be swept off the streets by making soliciting an offence. In 1958 alone nearly 20,000 charges were brought against prostitutes.[57] But, naturally, this did not end the trade. Those prostitutes with an up-market clientèle began operating from home, others simply shifted their 'patch' from the West End to new hunting grounds such as Notting Hill. Powis Square, in the Colville area, was teeming with brothels. George Clark remembers that 'the whole of the area was full of seedy low life. Not for nothing did Tiger Lil, who was perhaps the "Madame" of them all and who queened it over every prostitute in sight live in Colville Square, untouched by the police, untouchable almost.'[58]

Notting Hill appeared to breed celebrities in the fifties. Two local prostitutes rose in the early 1960s to the heights of fame: Christine Keeler and Mandy Rice Davies.[59] They used to go on nocturnal expeditions to a Shebeen in Powis Square, fishing for trade. Keeler lived in Notting Hill with a West Indian, John Edgecombe, before leaving him to live with Stephen Ward. Later, she returned to the Colville area to cohabit with another West Indian, 'Lucky' Gordon.

Keeler and Davies illustrate the ties that bound the black community in Notting Hill with high society. There was a close and complicated social web that linked these two seemingly incongruous worlds. Stephen Ward acted as a pimp for Rachman, introducing him to Keeler and Davies who both became his mistresses. Rachman lavished gifts on them. Davies, who lived with him until his death in 1962, was given £100 'pocket-money' each week and on her seventeenth birthday Rachman presented her with a white Jaguar.[60] Typically, he also arranged a forged driving licence so she could drive under-age. Rachman and Davies were regular guests at Stephen Ward's cottage in Cleveden, which is where Christine Keeler first met the Conservative Minister, John Profumo. They would also spend evenings in basement clubs in Notting Hill. At a price, the doors of the club would be closed to all but their favourite West Indian friends, including King Dick and Baron Baker.

Among this mixture of social classes and trades racial distinctions seemed to lose their significance. As Michael de Freitas put it: 'Amongst the legion of hustlers no colour is recognised. Specialists work together and have no colour, whether their line is sex, housebreaking, bank robbery or pick-pocketing.'[61]

But in the outside world West Indians continued to be given the cold shoulder. Few people who lived outside Notting Hill or areas like it could have appreciated how difficult it was to make ends meet. 'Life really hard for the boys in London,' wrote Samuel Selvon in 1956:

Those rich people who live in Belgravia and Knightsbridge and up in Hampstead and those other plush places, they would never believe what it's like in a grim place like Harrow Road or Notting Hill. Those people who have cars, or go to the theatre and ballet in the West End, who attend *premières* with the royal family, they don't know nothing about hustling two pound of brussel sprouts and half-pound potato, or queueing up for fish and chips in the smog.[62]

When Horace Ove left his middle-class family in the West Indies to come to Britain he did not expect to have to live in a poky, dirty bedsit in the worst part of London. Indeed, the first time that he ever experienced poverty was when he arrived in the Mother Country. 'I used to write back to my mother in Trinidad saying how great it was here, because I didn't want her to worry about me. So when my mother came and saw England for herself she had a terrible shock. For the whole of the first day she couldn't stop crying.'[63]

Nevertheless, the West Indians managed to keep their spirits high, comforting themselves with the thought that racial hostility and prejudice would soon die a natural death. Then they would be fully accepted as equals within British society. As A.G. Bennett put it in 1954: 'This is the Mother Country as we all know, and that's why she beat our backsides as only a mother could.'[64]

5
Keeping Britain White

In November 1954 the right-wing Labour politician, John Hynd, proposed that immigration should be regulated. He argued that only those West Indians suited to the economic needs of the country should be allowed into Britain.[1] Hynd received the enthusiastic backing of a small group of MPs from both sides of the House: Harry Hynd (Labour, Accrington); Notting Hill's MP, George Rogers (Labour, North Kensington); Norman Pannell (Conservative, Kirkdale); and most important Cyril Osborne (Conservative, Louth).

Osborne was the ring-leader of this lobby. Stock-broker and company director, he was something of a maverick within the Conservative party. In the early 1950s his was a lone voice, but as the decade progressed he converted more and more politicians to his cause. Between 1954 and 1958 Osborne orchestrated innumerable debates on the issue of immigration, arguing that the unrestricted entry of black people was a threat to the country's moral, social and economic well-being.[2] Never a very subtle speaker, he talked in terms of the spectre of shiploads of lepers arriving from Africa and of a 'coffee-coloured Britain'. When asked whether he would turn away black people from British ports if they had tuberculosis he replied: 'No, of course I would not, but I would not let them get as far as the ports.'[3] By 1955 he had generated enough support within the Conservative Party to pass a resolution through

the policy-making body of the Party – the Central Council –
approving by a narrow margin the call for immigration controls
which would allow the deportation of convicted criminals and
stowaways from the colonies.[4]

For such an extreme right-winger, Osborne had very odd
bedfellows within the anti-immigration lobby. In 1955 the
biennial delegates' conference of the Transport and General
Workers Union passed a resolution recognising the 'grave
situation which is revealed by uncontrolled immigration'. The
conference called on government to pass legislation to restrict
immigration and to increase capital investment in the West
Indies to eliminate the need for emigration to Britain.[5]

Despite such wide-ranging support, Osborne had no chance
of getting immigration control onto the statute book without
the backing of government. The first government to discuss
immigration had been the Attlee administration in 1950. In
June that year the Home Secretary Chuter Ede, George Isaacs,
Minister of Labour, and the Secretary of State for the Colonies
James Griffiths, met to discuss the immigration of colonial subjects. They considered in private a number of possible methods
of controlling the entry of black people, including a power to
bar unemployed migrants and to deport those convicted of a
serious offence or attempting to create industrial unrest. But
the Labour Government was nervous about implementing these
proposals, aware that they were bound to provoke uproar, both
within Britain and her colonies. It would be far too obvious
that a concealed colour test was being imposed, as the powers
taken would be applied most often to black people.[6] So they
decided not to pursue the matter further, fearing that it was
too controversial to handle.

The same three Ministers met the following year in the presence of Aneurin Bevan, the Health Minister and architect of the
National Health Service, to consider drafting a Bill to restrict
the entry of stowaways. Again they decided against immediate
action, this time because they felt that the influx of black people
was so limited that 'the present extent of the problem would not
justify recommending legislation'. However, they did agree to
reconsider the whole issue of immigration if black people started
entering on a 'significant scale' and the Secretary of State for
the Colonies said that he was watching the matter carefully.[7]

The Conservative Government that ousted Attlee in 1951 carried on the debate where Labour had left off. The Conservatives were concerned about the social and political affects of black people living in Britain. Could miscegenation, that is, sexual relations between blacks and whites, have a gradual effect on the 'national way of life'?[8] It was feared that West Indians were aggravating the housing crisis. The Colonial Secretary, Alan Lennox-Boyd, argued that the shortage of suitable accommodation resulted in large numbers of newcomers congregating in sub-standard houses and congested conditions and that this was liable to create tension and ill-feeling with other residents.[9] But the worst scenario that Ministers envisaged was that large-scale immigration would lead to the sorts of racial strife experienced in South Africa or America. They wondered whether Britain would see 'the creation of a plural way of society, with the prospect of race riots, colour-bar incidents, and the emergence of a set pattern of politics cutting across ordinary political issues?'[10]

The Government's answer to the threat of racial violence was to try and remove the source of irritation – black people. In 1953 the Cabinet made this explicit: 'How far trouble between white and black people can be avoided in future if the coloured community continues to increase is a matter for speculation. Against this background the question of whether it would be desirable to legislate to restrict the right of British subjects to enter the United Kingdom has to be considered.'[11]

Although these social and political preoccupations underpinned the debate, the overriding concern was economic. The 1948 Nationality Act meant that if unemployment returned, the Government would have no right to deport unwanted West Indian workers, which greatly marred their attraction as a source of surplus labour. Moreover, if black people themselves became unemployed it was within their rights to draw National Assistance. As the Secretary of State for the Colonies, Oliver Lyttleton, put it in 1954: 'I think we must look very seriously into whether some conditions are not necessary in the United Kingdom, if there is to be any means of controlling the increasing flow of colonial people who come here largely to enjoy the benefit of the welfare state.'[12]

At first the Government focused its attentions on trying to control black labour from within the country. In 1953 the

Home Office set up a confidential working party to report on possible ways of restricting the employment of black people who were already living in Britain. The most popular proposal was to step up discrimination at the labour exchanges, but Ministers felt that this would be too indiscreet and, in any event, it was unlikely to be effective because black people could always by-pass the labour exchanges and approach employers directly. The Cabinet concluded that regulating black labour through internal mechanisms would not suffice. The only other solution was immigration control, equivalent to erecting a giant colour bar right around the shores of Britain, like a castle moat. 'The conclusion must be that effective steps to reduce the number of coloured people seeking employment must be directed to reducing the number entering the United Kingdom for that purpose.'[13]

But how were they to keep black, and only black people, from entering the country? Ministers were open in their admiration of other white governments which had already implemented legislation of this sort. In Canada a quota system had been introduced, limiting the numbers of Indian, Pakistani and Ceylonese immigrants. New Zealand was slightly more stealthy: a person of 'non European' race and colour had to possess an official permit, which was rarely granted. Australia was most disingenuous. Anyone wishing to live and work there had to pass a dictation test in a European language. An English-speaking Indian could be tested in French, and a French speaker from West Africa in English.[14]

The British Government also scrutinised the American immigration system. Ministers clearly envied the McCarran-Walter Act of 1952 which put a quota on the number of West Indians entering the United States to work. The British Ambassador in Washington remarked: 'As for the British West Indies, the fact is that would-be immigrants are all in practice negroes. It seems to us very understandable that Americans should want to limit the flow of negro immigrants where practicable.'[15] What appealed most to the British was that the McCarran-Walter Act gave the US authorities the power to select the youngest, fittest and healthiest West Indian workers. In contrast, the British Government had no power to turn away any West Indians and this aroused increasing anxiety as the decade progressed, especially as from 1955 West Indian men began to be joined by their dependents – women, children and elderly parents who were regarded as a non-productive drain on the economy.

West Indians wishing to work in the USA had to undergo a rigorous medical examination before being offered a visa. This included urine tests and anal examinations, and their fingerprints were taken. Once passed by an employers' representative they were told to strip and, carrying only an identification card, sent from room to room, where they were further examined by medical and other technicians. According to the Colonial Office 'The spirit in which a man is processed is that the slightest evidence of a condition which might make him physically unable to perform a good day's work is cause for summary rejection.'[16]

Despite admiration for American procedures, the Government was aware that restricting the entry of black people was a highly sensitive issue. It smacked of segregation and apartheid, and would arouse liberal opposition in Britain. The *New Statesman* wrote in 1954 that 'Restrictions (which to serve their purpose would have to discriminate against coloured people) would be morally indefensible. They would be tantamount to branding the Queen's black subjects as second-class citizens'.[17]

Immigration control would also be very unpopular with the black colonial peoples against whom it would be directed. This was a matter of some concern to the Government, preoccupied as it was with preserving Britain's economic, political and 'moral' influence over the Empire. As colony after colony moved towards independence, Britain needed an alternative forum through which she could retain indirect control over her ex-colonial territories. The obvious vehicle for this was the Commonwealth, which Britain was desperate to expand as a balance to the rise in power of America and the Soviet Union.

Although Britain made sure that her colonies joined the Commonwealth on achieving independence, could she be certain that they would not eventually transfer their allegiances to one or other of the two new superpowers? The Colonial Office advised caution in Britain's handling of the period of de-colonisation, urging the Government to avoid any action that would alienate the colonies and weaken the ties that bound them to the Mother Country. Any curtailment of entry rights would hardly have been diplomatic at such a sensitive moment. Norman Manley, Jamaica's Chief Minister and head of the People's National Party, plainly stated his opposition to immigration control. In 1955 he said any attempt to restrict entry would raise 'very serious difficulties' and expressed surprise that a nation of 50 million should be so preoccupied with just 10,000 West Indian immigrants.[18] This was enough to convince the Colonial Secretary Alan Lennox-Boyd that if immigration control was necessary at least it should be strictly non-discriminatory.[19]

But other Cabinet Ministers disagreed. Lord Swinton, the Commonwealth Relations Secretary, said that he was 'not convinced that the legislation need be non-discriminatory in form'. Restrictions should be applied to 'only the particular class of immigrants which we have in mind'.[20] A senior official involved in the discussions was more blunt: 'The immigration control would be deliberately designed to hit impecunious "blacks" from the colonies and no-one else. The plain fact is that that would be the intention and it would be quite impossible to conceal it. My personal view is that this would probably be the lesser evil; but it would be criticised by so-called "liberals".'[21]

However, those who argued for openly discriminatory legislation ran against the grain. The general consensus was that immigration controls should not relate specifically to black people. But there was a problem about this too: non-discriminatory legislation would set a trap which would catch not only black people from the colonies, but also *white* people from the so-called 'Old Commonwealth' – Australia, New Zealand, Canada, Rhodesia and South Africa. The British Government had no desire to exclude white Commonwealth citizens and was unhappy about the potential strain this would put on Britain's relations with these countries.[22]

So the Government was left with an impossible task – to frame non-discriminatory immigration legislation that would apply only to black people. Surprisingly, they managed to hit on some suggestions. The first idea was to make it more difficult for black people to obtain passports in the colonies themselves.[23] The Home Secretary, David Maxwell-Fyfe, proposed in 1954 that even if black people did acquire passports, they could effectively be stopped from entering Britain by immigration officers at sea- and airports. A general law could be passed which in theory would require all new arrivals to satisfy immigration officers that they could maintain themselves without depending on public funds. Ministers expected that in practice black people would seldom pass this test.[24] The beauty of this system was that it would avoid the need to publicly define the type of people the Government wished to exclude. It was agreed that complete discretion would be given to immigration officers to refuse anyone whose entry would appear to be 'undesirable in the public interest' although that discretion would, of course, be exercised in accordance with the directions of the Secretary of State.[25] To minimise inconvenience caused to white visitors, immigration officers would be concentrated only at those ports at which the West Indians normally arrived. Other ports would only be checked if they were being used as entry points for 'unwanted immigrants.'[26]

Another suggestion popular with Ministers was a system of work permits for all immigrants. Employers wishing to import workers would have to apply for an official permit. This would appear to apply equally to all prospective immigrants, black or white, but the Government believed that there would be 'few cases in which employers would wish to import coloured workers'. Alternatively, permits could be reserved just for skilled immigrant workers. The Government thought this would be an even more subtle and effective means of restricting the entry of black people, because it was still thought that most West Indians were unskilled.[27]

The snag in the permit system was that it was unlikely to restrict the entry of black people at a time of full employment, such as the 1950s, when any workers, irrespective of race, were in demand. As a covering measure, the Government also proposed that immigration controls should be linked to housing, a commodity in much shorter supply. Prospective immigrants would have to show that they had somewhere to live before being allowed into the country. Again, this would appear to apply to all immigrants, but in practice blacks would find it much more difficult to secure accommodation than whites. The only difficulty with this form of control that Ministers could anticipate was that it relied on the co-operation of local housing authorities who could foil the scheme by choosing to offer accommodation impartially.[28]

In 1955 all these proposals were assembled in a draft Immigration Bill which proposed restricting entry to those who could prove that they had both a job and a home to go to. But the Cabinet sat on the Bill, unable to decide whether to introduce it. By 1956 some Ministers were arguing that it was time to act, before unemployment crept back. The 'open door' policy for British subjects had grown up, they said, when there was 'no danger of a coloured invasion'. But now the circumstances had changed. 'If no control were imposed now, we might be faced with the need for urgent action when it had already become too late.'[29]

But other Ministers argued that West Indian labour was still indispensable. 'There is no doubt,' reported a special Cabinet committee in 1956, 'that the West Indians already in this country have up to the present made a very useful contribution to the labour force, and there is no embarrassing problem on this score yet. So long as employment continues at its present very high rate, the arrival of further drafts of immigrants to fill low-paid manual jobs seems likely to ease rather than exacerbate the labour situation.'[30]

Ironically, as this comment suggests, the possibility of restricting black immigration was being discussed at a time when labour was still being actively sought. Indeed, London Transport only started recruiting workers in the West Indies in 1956, a year after the Immigration Bill was drafted. This highlights the fact that the Government regarded black people as an encumbrance even before they had outlived their economic utility. But Ministers were forced to temper their desire to curb black immigration because they were aware that it would be extremely difficult to justify at a time when labour was in such demand.

Ministers comforted themselves with the thought that immigration had not, as yet, harmed the 'national way of life'. 'There seems to be little evidence of inter-breeding,' said one unidentified Cabinet Member, although he appeared slightly more concerned about political developments. 'It is not impossible that in time the vote of the coloured population might achieve a significance out of proportion to its size in industrial towns,' he said.[31]

With the majority in the Cabinet satisfied that the usefulness of the West Indians continued to outweigh any potential disadvantages, the conclusion reached by these confidential Cabinet discussions in 1956 was that the draft Bill should be shelved until a more appropriate moment. For the time being the Government was content to let things ride. 'The ordinary people of this country seem to be by no means intolerant of coloured people. There appears to be little prospect of race riots or colour bar incidents on grounds of race alone.'[32] It added: 'But there is always the special risk that some particularly dastardly crime involving a coloured man might touch off trouble of this kind.'[33]

Only two years later it was the 'particularly dastardly crime' of nine white youths that sparked off race riots in Notting Hill.

6

The Beginning of Anger

The 1950s were said to herald the age of affluence. Wartime scarcity was gradually eased as people began to enjoy the fruits of victory. Production and consumption boomed and more people than ever before tasted the delights of a consumer society: wirelesses, record players, televisions, hoovers, electric toasters, refrigerators. It was like spring, or a renaissance, a fresh start symbolised by the Festival of Britain to which over eight million visitors flocked in 1951.[1]

It is also remembered as the decade when youth burst out into its own. Suddenly, young people were earning a living wage and spending it on themselves. The new concept of the teenager grew up around young people who previously would have been regarded as either old children or young adults – minors with no identity of their own. Now teenagers could afford to stand up for themselves, neither prohibited by the child's lack of spending power, nor inhibited by adult responsibilities. On film James Dean and in music the explosion of Rock'n'Roll epitomised a new youth culture. Bill Haley and the Comets burst musical conventions with 'Rock around the clock' in 1956. The 1950s also heard the softer sounds of Frank Sinatra, Doris Day and Alma Cogan, and Elvis Presley who in 1958 alone produced four unforgettable numbers: 'Hound dog', 'All shook up', 'Jailhouse Rock', and 'Hard-hearted woman'. England had her own home-made version of Elvis, an ex-merchant seaman who started out in the early 1950s as Tommy Hicks, a singer in London's seedy basement dives, and ended the decade the superstar all-round entertainer Tommy Steele.[2]

In short the early and mid fifties saw a Britain beginning to emerge from wartime austerity and daring to consider herself entering a new age of affluence. But all generalisations about Britain's affluence and new mood obscure as much as they illuminate. Consumer luxuries were still alien to many people, as indeed were bare essentials. In 1958, 35 per cent of Britain's households had no bath and nearly one third had no access to hot water.[3] Until 1953 rationing was in force and even more severe than at the height of the war. Meat, bacon, butter, cheese, tea, sugar and sweets were all strictly rationed and unless you could benefit from the flourishing black market you simply went without. 'At the time things weren't very pleasant for anybody. Times were hard'.[4]

Of course, just how hard life was in the fifties depended on the individual's background and livelihood. For families living in the neighbourhood of Notting Dale, times were extremely hard indeed. The Dale, which forms part of Notting Hill, is a small area to the west of the Colville area. It has its own distinct character and history and it played a central role in the events that were to unfold in Notting Hill. Unlike the Colville area where most of the West Indians lived, with its tall Victorian buildings, Notting Dale had always been a working-class area with houses to match. Rows of tenements lined the maze of streets and back-alleys around Latimer Road station. Some had two storeys but others were cottages built during the 1870s to house the navvies who constructed London's railways.[5]

Notting Dale began life as a slum and ended life as a slum. Until most of the area was knocked down in the late 1960s it was one of the most derelict pockets in London. In the 1950s London was scarred with neighbourhoods like Notting Dale, lying tucked away just out of sight of the high street, caught between the age of affluence and Dickens' England.

Dickens had, in fact, described the Dale in 1850 as 'a plague spot scarcely equalled for insalubrity by any other in London'.[6] In the nineteenth century the area was called the 'Potteries', after the kilns where the soft local clay soil was cut and fired to make bricks. But in the middle of the century a man

called Samuel Lake settled there as a refugee from the West
End, having been hounded out because of his various shady
activities. Lake was the Victorian version of Rachman. Instead
of housing prostitutes and West Indians in return for exorbitant
rents he crammed pig keepers and their animals into hovels,
with the understanding that as long as they paid him promptly
they could do as they liked in return, and he'd see that nobody
meddled with them.[7]

Under Lake's system of housing management the Potteries,
now called the 'Piggeries', was turned into an enormous pigsty.
At one point there were some 3,000 pigs and 1,000 people
living together in 260 shacks.[8] The pigs were fed on left-overs
collected by the women and children from West End hotels, the
offal being boiled down in open vats which impregnated the air
with putrid smells. Drainage was almost impossible due to the
impermeable clay soil and the whole area was covered with open
sewers and pools of excrement. One of these pools was so large
that it was dubbed the 'Ocean' – a vast expanse nearly an acre
in diameter covered in filthy slime and bubbling with poisonous
gases caused by the drainage of pigsties and privies into it.[9]
Ramshackle cottages, inhabited primarily by Irish families,
lay right on the edge of the Ocean and in some instances the
floors had partially collapsed into the effluent. Families would
sleep on straw mattresses on the dry side of the room, opposite
the gently lapping, stagnant waters.[10] The area had one of the
highest mortality rates in London and in 1848 an epidemic of
cholera broke out, lowering the average life expectancy of the
inhabitants to eleven years and seven months.[11]

Although the pigs were cleared from the Dale by the end
of the nineteenth century, it continued to be one of the most
run-down areas of London, with extreme overcrowding, poverty
and a transient population. The economically and socially
rejected congregated there. Nearly a quarter of the population
of the Dale was Irish, together with numerous prostitutes and
tramps and fifty gypsy families who used to winter there. The
population ebbed and flowed along with the availability of
work, much of which was service employment in the wealthy
households which lay only a few streets south in Holland
Park. Women were the main earners, working as servants or
laundry maids, and it was a standing joke locally that men

moved there for the purpose of being kept by their wives.[12] Men who had jobs worked in casual trades as coster-mongers, organ-grinders, rag-and-bone men, street hawkers, flower-sellers, ice-cream vendors or petty thieves.[13]

By the 1950s Notting Dale had become more stable, facilitated by improvements in housing and the growth of steady employment opportunities in the 1920s that followed in the wake of the railway boom. Many of the gypsy families had left their caravans to live in cottages, and the movement of families into and out of the area had become less frequent. This gave the area a closer feeling of community. Jean Maggs, who was a teenager in the fifties, lived in the same house as her parents, grandparents and great-grandparents before her. Everybody knew each other. There were no strangers and if she wanted to visit a friend she would walk straight into the house using the key that was kept on a piece of string by the front door.[14]

The Dale was like a village, with its own customs and loyalties. Notting *Hill* to the inhabitants of Notting *Dale* meant a conglomerate of different villages: Notting Hill Gate where the 'toffs' lived; 'the Town' to the east of Ladbroke Grove which included the Colville area where many West Indians lived; and the Dale itself. Further to the west were Shepherds Bush and Hammersmith and further east, Paddington. Each village kept its distance from the others, with remarkably little contact between them. Jean Maggs' grandparents never spoke to each other, because one family came from the Dale and the other from the Bush. 'My parents had a mixed marriage you see,' she jokes. Her father, who came from Shepherds Bush and made his living by picking pockets at the races, refused to work with men from Notting Dale.

People from the Dale also kept aloof from the Town. If Jean Maggs went 'down the Pally' on a Saturday night with friends from the other side of Ladbroke Grove her mother would get worried and tell her to be careful because 'you can't trust the mob from the Town'. 'Even today Town people and Dale people keep themselves to themselves,' Maggs says. 'Don't forget,' she adds laughing, 'I married a bloke from Bristol 25 years ago and I still haven't been forgiven.'[15]

The word 'village' connotes idyllic hamlets in the countryside, nestled among rolling hills. But there was nothing 'villagey' in this sense about Notting Dale, which was more like a bomb site in the fifties than a rural haven. A V2 rocket landed in the centre of the area during the war, leaving patches of wasteland covered in debris where families lived in pre-fabricated concrete shacks. The tenements that were left standing after the war were desperately overcrowded, with three generations living in the same house – grandparents upstairs, parents in the middle and children in the basement. Jean Maggs' two-storey tenement wasn't very overcrowded, she says – it only housed 16 people; in other tenements there were up to 40 people crammed together. 'We weren't too badly off compared to some because we had two rooms to share between seven of us.'[16]

It was rare for houses to have bathrooms so the people used to go to the local baths to wash themselves and their clothes. Some houses had large copper or tin baths which would be put in front of the fire and one after the other the family would bathe in it, using the same water. But many houses were so damp that inside baths were avoided.

The only sense that could be made out of Macmillan's contention that they had never had it so good, was that the 1950s weren't quite as bad as the 1940s. During the fifties the inhabitants of Notting Dale were still living in poverty of a different shade and the fruits of the age of affluence – wirelesses, record players, televisions and cars – were enjoyed by very few. Most people lived hand to mouth and anything left over at the end of the week was spent in pubs. Apart from pubs the most common services in the area were pawnbroker shops. Jean Maggs remembers calling their pawnbroker 'Uncle'. Her father used to take his only suit out every Saturday, wear it on Sunday, and then take it back to Uncle on Monday. Pawnshops were an essential part of the local economy, a safeguard against having no money at the end of the month when the rent was due. As with the West Indians in Rachman's houses, if you didn't pay your rent in Notting Dale you were flung out onto the street. When Jean Maggs' father fell ill with cancer they had to pawn all their furniture to keep their landlord at bay.[17]

Although work was plentiful it tended to be unskilled and poorly paid. Women worked as cleaners or kitchen-hands in the smart houses in Holland Park, just as they had a hundred years before. Notting Dale, like the Colville area, also had a flourishing trade in prostitution. The Methodist minister David Mason remembers visiting a woman in a shabby house in Bramley Road, in the heart of the Dale, who wanted a baby baptised: 'I was wearing my dog-collar and everything. I knocked on the door and then went in and to my astonishment it was like a palace inside, with a bar: it was a high-class brothel. All these city gents sitting around in their pin-stripes. She took me into her room, and there I was sitting on this bed, wearing my dog-collar, obviously on the spot where she did her job!'[18]

Men worked as railway labourers, builders, grocers or carpet-beaters and many, like Jean Maggs' father, supplemented their meagre incomes with a bit of petty crime. Once in a blue moon someone would struggle out of the poverty trap. This tiny patch of London, with only 2,000 inhabitants, spawned in the 1950s not only a big-time bank robber, Joe Cannon, but also two top-class sportsmen: the footballer Alan Mullery, of Fulham and Spurs, who went on to captain England, and John Murray the English wicket-keeper.[19]

For the rest, the hardship of making ends meet was balanced by a strong sense of community. Everyone was poor and everyone helped each other. As John Garrett, who worked as a coal-man in the fifties and has lived all his life in the Dale, put it: 'If a few boys were being chased by the coppers they would run into someone's house, climb over the wall and into someone else's back yard. We knew everyone so it didn't matter. It made the coppers' life a misery!'[20] Every year children would be treated to 'charabanc outings' to the sea by a local charity. On hot summer nights women would sit outside on special seats built into their front porches, and at weekends there were hop-picking outings to the country which was hard work but the closest most people got to a holiday. The first time that Mary O'Connor, who still lives in Latimer Road, enjoyed a non-working holiday was in 1957, when she was taken to the seaside at the age of 41.[21]

Young people used to entertain themselves by going to the Royalty picture palace on Sunday afternoons, dances at the town hall or boxing at the local public baths. In the summer they would catch a bus to Battersea Park. There were also a couple of youth clubs in the area – the Dale club and the Rugby club, the latter set up by the public school of that name as a charitable gesture on behalf of the poor of Notting Dale. But although teenagers were supposed to have spending power in the 1950s, in the Dale their wages were largely eaten up by family debts and obligations and their life could not be called exciting. Not much could be done with only a few shillings, and many teenagers spent their leisure hours roaming the streets in search of action.

Notting Dale in the 1950s remained a fairly homogeneous white area, with relatively few West Indians living in Bramley Road and Blechynden Street near Latimer Road tube station. Ironically, having started life as a home to immigrant Irish and gypsy people, Notting Dale had developed into a settled and closed community, virulently hostile to 'foreigners'. By the 1950s it was the antithesis of the Colville area which lay just across Ladbroke Grove only half-a-mile to the east. In many ways, the Colville area was in the 1950s what Notting Dale had been fifty years before – a run-down, transient area with a variegated migrant population. Perhaps it reminded the residents of Notting Dale of a past which they pre-ferred to forget. At any rate, as the decade progressed the white inhabitants of Notting Dale became increasingly antagonistic towards the black inhabitants of the neighbouring 'village'.

In 1956 a poll was conducted on the attitudes of 300 white people from six different districts of England and Scotland. It showed that only a minority – 4 per cent – believed that black people were 'uncivilised' and less than one tenth were of the opinion that all mixing between the races should be avoided.[22] But the significance of that 10 per cent should not be under-estimated, bolstered as it was by machinations within the corridors of power. The Government kept silent in public about the arrival of the West Indians; silent, too, about the propaganda its own back-benchers like Cyril Osborne were spreading about the 'coloured invasion'. Meanwhile, more people left Britain for Australia each year than arrived from the West Indies. While so much fuss was being made in the early fifties about the arrival of a few thousand West Indians annually, some 30,000 Britons emigrated to Australia every month. During the fifties as a whole 912,000 people left Britain for the antipodes, while only 482,000 immigrated. Even among the numbers of Britain's new arrivals there were more whites from Canada, Australia and Ireland than blacks from the West Indies and Asia.[23] But the public remained ignorant about these population movements because the figures were rarely publicised.

Locally, some politicians were encouraging unwelcoming attitudes towards West Indians. The Labour MP for Notting Hill was George Rogers, a former railway clerk and the Opposition whip for London from 1954. He was one of Cyril Osborne's earliest supporters in the lobby against black immigration. The Methodist minister David Mason remembers that, 'There wasn't a black face in the Labour Party. Rogers lived in Sussex, ex-directory, interested in spiritualism and painting. The local Party was hopeless, absolutely hopeless; Gaitskell wouldn't attend its social functions, on the grounds that it was disgraceful.'[24] 'I was perplexed at the time about so-called British socialism,' says Barbadian Ivan Weekes . 'I still am perplexed now after thirty years. As a boy I believed in British socialism. But there you had George Rogers, a Labour MP, who didn't want to know anything about black people. He was concerned that the white working-class people around here voted him back in.'[25]

As for the other local institution, the Church of England, David Mason reports: 'There were numerous churches in the area, but oh dear, they were just supplying the Victorian church games, as though it was still the 1890s, arguing about baptism or what robes priests should wear. The social issues – none of them were ready for it.'[26] The Church was not universally backward on race issues. Father Trevor Huddleston, who was deeply involved in anti-apartheid activities in South Africa until recalled by his church superiors in 1955, was one of the most vociferous opponents of immigration control in this country. In 1958 he was Prior of the Community of the Resurrection's house in Holland Park, just south of Notting Hill. But other clergymen were less enlightened. Ivan Weekes recalls going to the All Saints Church in the heart of the Colville area one Sunday morning. The vicar went up to him at the end of the service, smiling. 'It's nice to see you, Ivan,' he said, 'but I'd prefer not to see you next Sunday. Of course, *I* don't mind, but my congregation might – they're not used, you know, to seeing black faces.'[27] Many deeply religious West Indians stopped attending church, so disillusioned had they become. They were disgusted by young white children or adults sitting in the pew behind, whispering about them in the most offensive and irreverent language.[28]

The failure of the Church to confront prejudice as a moral issue hurt not only the West Indians, however. It also left white people in the wilderness. Indeed, the silence of the Church and of politicians spoke louder than words. For in the absence of an informed political or moral debate, white people developed their own theories about blacks, often based on hearsay and conjecture.

At first white people were confused and perplexed by the newcomers, many having never set eyes on black people before. Even by 1961, 65 per cent of the population had never worked with blacks.[29] They knew nothing about who these strangers were, or where they had come from, as was shown by the kinds of questions they would ask West Indians: 'How come you speak such good English?' 'What's life in the jungle like?' 'Do you believe in devils?'[30] Margaret Garrett, a white woman living then as now in Notting Dale, accepts that she was ignorant in those days: 'We had no black people in our school. The only black man I ever saw was a bloke who sold Indian toffee. It was really quite sad – people saying blacks ate Kit-e-Kat and were dirty.'[31]

The West Indians themselves were bemused by English attitudes towards them. As one Jamaican woman put it: 'They think all coloured people are Jamaicans and they think all Jamaicans are beggars.'[32] The West Indians were very surprised that although they knew much about the English from their contact in the Caribbean, many English people here knew next to nothing about them. Sometimes people would come up to them in the street and rub their hands to see if the dirt came off.[33] Ivan Weekes remembers that people used to look at him as though he were a little monkey. 'They didn't know what had hit them. They used to ask me if Barbados is part of Jamaica. They knew the empire existed from Lord Beaverbrook in the *Express*, but that was about all.'[34]

With no information readily available about the West Indians, white people latched onto the easiest and most accessible explanations. From before recorded time black people have been regarded as alien beings by whites. They were branded devils, monsters and apes, and the Church had taught that their blackness was God's curse on Ham for looking on his father's nakedness as he lay drunk in his tent.

With the advent of slavery equally ignorant stereotypes were developed to justify treating black people like caged animals. Slave owners had to convince themselves and others that blacks were inferior and deserved to be exploited because they were not entirely human. At first, crude stereotypes were based on the theory that black people were descended from the coupling of monkeys and humans. Later, pseudo-scientific notions suggested that blacks were genetically inferior. Darwin's theory of evolution was bastardised to support the argument that some humans (white) had reached a higher evolutionary stage than others (black).[35]

By the early eighteenth century black people were thought of as intrinsically lazy, but cut out for hard labour.[36] The *Universal History* (1736–65) accused black people of promoting lust through living off the immoral earnings of prostitutes.[37] Even as early as 1764 a writer in the *London Chronicle* called for immigration control to prevent these 'spiteful, sullen and revengeful' people from coming to England. 'As they fill the places of so many of our own people, we are by this means depriving so many of them of the means of getting their bread, and thereby decreasing our native population in favour of a race whose mixture with us is disgraceful.'[38]

It is extraordinary how little these images changed over time. So forceful were they that by the beginning of the twentieth century they had become infused within British culture at every level. 'Younger white people were all prejudiced,' says Baron Baker. 'They were taught they were better than black people, so you couldn't expect any different from them. All of those *Ten Little Nigger* books labelled us even before they set eyes on us.'[39]

Children's books, as Baker suggests, were one medium for transmitting racial stereotypes. Take Enid Blyton's *The Three Golliwogs*, published in 1944, which would have been read by children who were young adults in 1958:

> There were once three golliwogs who were most unhappy in the nursery cupboard. None of the other toys liked them, because their mistress, Angela, didn't like their black faces.[40]

One was called 'Nigger', another 'Golly' and the third 'Woggie'. Poor little golliwogs, they were all so alike that nobody could tell them apart!

Katharine Tozer published a very popular children's story in 1935 called *The Wanderings of Mumfie*. One day Mumfie the elephant comes across a black man, John Gingerbread. 'Have you got any education?' Mumfie asks. 'No! massa, certainly not, sah!' 'Hem!' goes Mumfie. 'Well, John Gingerbread, have you seriously applied yourself to the task of scrubbing your face every day in order to get it a bit whiter?' 'Yes, boss,' says John Gingerbread.[41]

Whether or not children from Notting Hill read these stories, they picked up the idea that black people were different from a very early age. Jean Maggs remembers that as a child she was taught that if she saw a black man she should spit on the ground for luck.[42] In English schools Britain's black colonies and subjects were rarely discussed. Children were, of course, taught about the Empire but teachers focused, with few exceptions, on the roles of white European administrators, explorers, statesmen, soldiers, settlers and missionaries. In this picture black people lacked all identity or distinction and were characterised uniformly as 'natives'.[43]

Young children learnt to fear and dislike black people without ever having talked to one. An experiment conducted in 1953 introduced a classroom of white children to two black women teachers. At the start the children professed their open hatred for blacks, but after being taught for two weeks by the black women they almost unanimously agreed that they thought black people better, more likeable, civilised and better educated than 'other immigrant groups'. Black people were more like themselves than they had expected, they said, and they concluded that black people were every bit as good as them – except for their colour.[44]

Stereotypes of black people were also transmitted through the press. Even as early as 1949, only one year after the arrival of the *Empire Windrush*, Fleet Street was spreading the notion that black people relied on government benefits. The *Evening News*, for instance, carried an article called 'A Nice Pair of Socks for Eight-ball' which portrayed a black man with this curious name standing in front of an outfitter's shop, pondering which of the pairs of gaudy socks he is going to buy with his assistance money. The article claimed, ridiculously, that 65 per cent of all 'colonials' – a euphemism for black people

– in Britain were living off the Assistance Board.[45] As the 1950s progressed the tone of newspaper accounts became more shrill, lambasting black newcomers for orchestrating crime and prostitution rings.[46] Newspaper articles began spreading blatant lies about black people using the most emotive language. Images of water and drowning evoked fear and loathing in the reader: black people were 'swamping' Britain, there was a 'wave' of coloured immigrants, a 'flood' of foreigners. *'These Men Will Not Work'* screamed the *News Chronicle* in 1954. *'Coloured idlers alarm six cities. They live on public money.'* This article went on to claim that half the West Indian arrivals never made any effort to get work, but lived a life of luxury on the dole; and that blacks were the culprits in 90 per cent of all dangerous drug offences and in 80 per cent of all cases of living off prostitution – all of which was palpable nonsense.[47]

The poorest people living in the most run-down areas were particularly vulnerable to this sort of racist propaganda because they were the most economically and socially insecure, the most frustrated and the most angry. It was a volatile cocktail. Notting Dale had only just managed to drag itself out of Victorian poverty, and it would only have taken a spell of severe unemployment to push it back again. People were protective about their jobs and insular within their communities, talking in terms of 'locals' and 'foreigners', despite the fact that the original inhabitants of Notting Dale were themselves migrants.

Of course, West Indians were not the first immigrant group to suffer prejudice. Irish people living in the Dale from the early nineteenth century were never totally accepted and nor were Jewish people. A Jewish family living near Jean Maggs were constantly harassed.[48] Travelling families were another object of abuse.

Hostility made it very difficult for West Indians to find houses to rent in Notting Dale. White people from the Dale commented acerbically on the life-styles and characters of their black neighbours. With no knowledge of black people as individuals they saw them through stereotype-tinted glasses which, like fairground mirrors, distorted images of ordinary people into grotesque caricatures.

The first set of caricatures were employment-related. Black people were regarded as intrinsically inferior workers who could work hard ('like niggers') but whose place was at the bottom of the pile. The reason for this was said to be that they were either inherently or educationally backward. 'Basically the West Indians were very uneducated,' says Bob Davis who worked, then as now, as a policeman in Notting Hill:

> They were as thick as two short planks, educationally speaking. Which is why they gravitated to the minor jobs wasn't it – because they weren't capable of doing anything else. They *weren't*. I don't care what all the eggheads and educationalists and all the rest say. How can you get a bloke who's been a farmer growing bananas in Jamaica suddenly become an accountant – it doesn't happen does it? Nobody's disputing the fact they might have the intelligence to do these jobs, but you've got to educate them first.[49]

In fact, around 80 per cent of the West Indians had completed their schooling and 5 per cent of the men, 11 per cent of the women, had had further or higher education.[50] Although no figures are available, that would have compared favourably with the level of education in Notting Dale.

As we have seen, when unemployment crept back in 1956 black people were the first to lose their jobs. By 1958 over 8 per cent of black people in Britain – 17,000 – were jobless compared with only 2 per cent unemployment among whites.[51] Rumours began to spread that blacks were drawing more national assistance than whites. One of the white rioters in 1958 said: 'We were in the labour exchange the other day, three of us, and we're standing waiting for our pay and we see one darkie go up, he drew seven pounds something. Then we see six whites go up and they only draw three pounds! And its nearly all blacks down there except for the few whites.' But the same man also thought that blacks were given jobs instead of whites, because they worked for less pay.[52]

Unemployment never reached critical proportions in the 1950s and a more common resentment than 'They've come to take our jobs', was 'They've come to take our homes'. The housing crisis, especially in London, was a cause of great frustration for white people as well as black. Young couples postponed their marriages or lived with parents because they could find no place of their own. In a borough like Kensington, where the council was opposed on principle to public housing, young single people had virtually no hope of being offered a council house. But the council seemed too distant to blame for the housing crisis, especially as there was a scapegoat close at hand. When the inhabitants of Notting Dale saw white people being forced out of houses in the Colville area and black people moving in, they assumed that the West Indians were driving whites out of their homes. They did not know that Rachman and other landlords were orchestrating this change because they could extract higher rents from blacks. Similarly, they had no knowledge of the Government's housing policies and found it more comprehensible to blame the West Indians for the housing shortage. No matter that the West Indians were being charged exorbitant rents to live in dingy rooms. 'Housing – that was basically the problem. Youngsters getting married with nowhere to live and then the blacks started arriving and they took all the flats.'[53]

The conditions in which West Indians were forced to live reinforced prejudices. Regional government officials reported that objections to working with West Indians focused primarily on disapproval of their standard of living and the generally squalid surroundings in which black workers were most often to be found. 'The coloured community are said to live in very poor conditions,' an official wrote in 1953, 'described variously as primitive, squalid and deplorable. Many police reports say that the coloured people seem to live in these bad conditions from choice.'[54]

Peter Taylor who, as a white teenager living in Notting Dale, took part in the riots, thinks that the area deteriorated only when black people started arriving:

It was the blacks and foreigners that made the area a slum. Everybody had a dustbin in those days. But the blacks didn't use it; they flung the stuff out of the top window and expected the dustmen to clear it up. It got to the stage where you could walk down the street and tell the houses where the black men lived. They were in a terrible state, awful. Broken windows never replaced. Filthy rotten curtains with holes in them.[55]

White people raised objections to almost anything the West Indians did. The habit of sitting on front door steps in summer, though practiced by white women in Notting Dale, was considered ground for opprobrium, as was leaving washing hanging out of windows, keeping curtains drawn and painting doors and windows in bright colours.[56] Police Constable Davis says:

> They behaved differently – they're noisy for a start. They don't live the same, they really don't. Well, now they've changed a lot, but in those days you could spot a Jamaican straight off a boat with his peg top trousers and his sky-blue suit, and a hat about this wide, dancing in the street at three o'clock in the morning as pissed as a rat. And then, when people came and said to them 'Go home!', they got all upset because that's the way they always behave. 'What we doing wrong man?' they'd say. Well, at four o'clock in the morning the average Joe in the street could tell them a lot of things that they were doing wrong, but it all eventually boiled down to the same thing: You're here! That's the easiest way to solve it, isn't it – make sure they're not.[57]

Racial discrimination and prejudice fed each other symbiotically, like a self-fulfilling prophecy. Black people were barred from reasonable accommodation because landlords thought them dirty and primitive then, when they were driven into slums like the Colville area, this was taken as proof that they were little better than animals. They were refused work because they were regarded as lazy then, when they were forced to rely on the dole, this was taken as confirmation of their indolence. If they did have work the fact that blacks were concentrated at the bottom of the employment ladder was used to support the argument that they were less able than white workers.

There was no logic to attitudes towards West Indians. They were criticised for taking lower wages than whites, then accused of being flash and ostentatiously wealthy. But how could West Indians be both poorly paid and rich? One man said: 'They live like dirt in private and like kings the rest of the time.'[58] Another said: 'Oh well, they work for lower wages so they can't get nicked for living off prostitutes.'[59] The West Indians were both idle good-for-nothings living off the state, and people who came to Britain to take our jobs. 'It's not often you see black men working, is it?' says Peter Taylor. After a pause he adds: 'All that talk about the blacks getting the worst jobs is all a load of bollocks – they got all the best paid jobs in London Transport.'[60]

One man said with unconscious irony: 'The darkies ride around in Rolls Royces and Cadillacs and there's my old man – works like a bleeding nigger and can't afford a Prefect.'[61]

But all these prejudices looked tame in comparison with the one burning hate that consumed the passions of so many young white men in the 1950s – sexual relations between white women and black men. A Gallup poll conducted shortly after the race riots found that the most common resentments expressed by whites were that blacks should not be allowed to compete equally for jobs (37 per cent) and that blacks should not be able to enter housing lists on the same conditions (54 per cent). But these were dwarfed by a startling 71 per cent of respondents who were opposed to racial intermarriage.[62]

Disapproval of *miscegenation* was rife at all levels of British society. The agony-aunt column of one glossy magazine, *Glamour*, advised a reader who was involved with a black man: 'Many coloured people are fine people, but they do come from a different race, with a very different background and upbringing. Besides, scientists do not yet know if it is wise for two such very different races as whites and blacks to marry, for sometimes children of mixed marriages seem to inherit the worst characteristics of each race.'[63]

At least this was accurate on one count – that some scientists were expounding most unscientific theories. As late as 1963, for instance, Dr Ernest Claxton, Assistant Secretary to the British Medical Association, asserted that chastity should be enforced among black people in Britain in order to minimise the risk of reproducing children of mixed blood which he thought was becoming an increasing problem.[64] Another medic, Dr Bertram, fellow of St John's College Cambridge and member of the Eugenics Society, wrote in 1958, just before the riots, that when a community dominated by one race is invaded by a small number of men of a different race those men tend to mate with women of inferior social and biological standing, thus limiting the prospects of their offspring.[65] These inflammatory views even touched the House of Lords, where Lord Elton – author of *The Unarmed Invasion*[66] – expressed similar ideas in suitably grandiose terms. 'History itself,' he said, 'has shown that not every form of inter-breeding is successful or desirable in every context and every area.'[67]

Notions about the undesirability of inter-racial breeding had become widely diffused by 1958. In Notting Dale, a woman interviewed after the riots whose daughter was living with a black man said: 'He's given her two little brown-skinned babies. Sweet they are, but I can't bear to look at them.'[68]

The sight of a mixed couple walking the streets of Notting Hill was anathema to many white people. Immediately after the riots white teenagers who took part in the disturbances were asked why they thought white women should be attracted to black men. 'First of all, for the money,' one said. 'Well I mean the darkies entertain them pretty well. They got plenty of stuff, plenty of drink, chuck a bit of dope in the drink and the girls want to stick with them.'[69] 'Just a lot of ponces live round there,' another young man said. 'I mean, it's not very nice to see a coloured bloke with a white girl out on the streets, is it? I don't mind white people doing it, but not black. We don't want a lot of half-castes running around do we. In my opinion they ought to be shot, the whole lot of them.'[70]

There was a common assumption that a white woman involved with a black man was bound to be a prostitute, as no 'respectable' woman would so demean herself. Needless to say, the West Indians found the suggestion that only prostitutes liked them highly offensive. 'If I was seen walking down the street with the Queen of England and nobody recognised who she was, it would be assumed she was a street girl.'[71] Baron Baker found the contention laughable, bearing in mind his friendship with Sarah Churchill.

Liaisons between white men and black women were tacitly accepted, but relationships between black men and white women were perceived as a threat. Perhaps this was because these mixed relationships challenged the control white men had over the opposite sex: in other words, what white men feared and hated most was not so much that black men liked their sisters but that their sisters liked black men.

Some women, albeit a minority, refused to be intimidated by their peers and openly flouted the mores against mixed relationships. They would be labelled 'white trash' and 'nigger lovers'. Other women were tempted to follow suit but were too afraid of the consequences. In Notting Dale very few white women mixed with West Indians and they were shunned and ostracised by their own family and friends if they did. Jean Maggs was one of the women who found the pressure too overbearing to resist. When her father discovered that she had talked to a black neighbour he refused to speak to her for two weeks and after that she eschewed the company of black men.[72]

Listening to Jean Maggs, one can begin to appreciate the terror that gripped Notting Dale. To ignorant white people, the West Indians were strange and peculiar beings who appeared to have materialised out of nowhere. They felt that their only securities in a hostile world – their community and their whiteness – were under siege. Looking back today, Jean Maggs now recognises how misguided she was. But back in 1958, still a teenager, she believed unquestioningly what she was told:

> It was our parents who drummed it into us and so we hated the blacks. They said they had come to take our jobs and our homes. I'm not prejudiced now, but I definitely was then. I was more frightened, I think, than prejudiced. My Dad, he was frightened too – we hadn't really seen or mixed with black people before. You had to live in this area to feel that fear.[73]

If the 1950s was the decade of Rock'n'Roll and the teenager it was also the era of the Teddy Boy, so called because his dress was cribbed from upper-class Edwardian fashion. Teddy Boys emerged from poor neighbourhoods in Elephant and Castle, south London, in 1953 and by the following year had spread to working-class districts throughout London and the provinces. Their trade-marks were greasy slick-backed hair in two styles – the 'Tony Curtis' look or the 'D.A.' (Duck's Arse) – sideboards, long velvet-lined frock-coats, bootlace ties, drainpipe trousers and four-inch solid corridor creepers.

By 1956 the Ted movement was in full swing. When the film *Blackboard Jungle* appeared that year featuring Bill Haley's 'Rock around the Clock' the Teds went wild. The phrase 'Rock'n'Roll riot' was coined to describe their Saturday night escapades: instead of rocking in their seats the Teds took to ripping them up, which was much more fun.[74]

The media latched onto the advent of the Teddy Boys, portraying it as a symbol of the breakdown in society's moral fabric and the collapse of law and order. Even though Teddy Boys came from, and were a part of, the poorest working-class communities in London, commentators explained the 'Teddy Boy phenomenon', as it was called, as a side-effect of the age of affluence. The implication was that working-class youths had become spoiled by being given too much money, and now they were misbehaving. As one criminologist put it: 'The Teddy Boy gangs – and this is the disturbing point – are a direct product of today, a by-product of a new economic revolution which has put spending money on a scale not known before into the pockets of working-class boys and girls.'[75]

Because of hysterical reactions to the Teddy Boy cult, it is difficult to tell whether youth violence really did increase during the decade. Police statistics certainly suggest it did. The number of teenagers arrested in London for indictable offences in 1958 was twice as many as in 1953. The Metropolitan Police Commissioner wrote in his report for 1958 that 'the country has, in the past few years, become conscious of a growing indifference of a section of the adolescent population for order and authority amounting in many areas to open defiance.'[76]

Part of this alarming rise in the crime statistics may have been based on an actual increase in crime, but part of the rise could have been accounted for by greater police activity against young people. The Teddy Boys were probably no more violent than their fathers or grandfathers before them. In the nineteenth century young men from the west London villages of Hammersmith and Paddington used to hold regular gang-fights on the neutral territory of Notting Hill.[77] But the terrifying image that the press and the police gave to the Teddy Boys in the fifties meant that they were put under a state of public siege. Ostracised and barred from cafés and cinemas, working-class teenagers were pushed onto the streets, fired with renewed anger and frustration. The authorities certainly achieved what they had set out to do, namely, to protect private property. But there was a heavy price to pay, for the Teddy Boys reacted by turning against the next obvious target – people.

Gangs of Teddy Boys developed a new form of entertainment: smashing up cafés owned by Cypriots – 'Cyps' as they called them. 'It was the excitement!' said one youth after the riots: 'I've seen our blokes heave a fellow they didn't know through a plate-glass window. I tell you, I couldn't stop laughing. One time six of us went to get one of the blacks; I didn't know what

he'd done but anyway he was a Spade. We just don't care.'[78]
'Well, it'd start with fists, then somebody'd get rough. We used
bottles and chains and hammers,' said another. Gangs would
make special excursions to London's East End, to Commercial
Road, to beat up Cypriots. Or they would attack black people,
shouting at them in the streets 'You black bastards' to try to
provoke them. 'We'd often go for the blacks. We don't like them,
we hate them.'[79]

Crime and fighting were a part of the local culture of
Notting Dale. According to David Mason, one pub in the
Dale was a 'thieves' kitchen'. 'It was a notorious place where
criminals met; the police knew it, we knew it, it was that sort
of neighbourhood.'[80] Drinking was an essential characteristic of
the area, with over fifteen pubs within the radius of half-a-mile;
a local magistrate described it as the haunt of every drunkard
in England.[81] In the 1950s, unlicensed bars, aptly called
'Mushroom clubs' started popping up all over. Word would
spread round the Dale that a club would be open that night
and drinking would continue late into the night, but by the
next morning the club would have disappeared without trace.
Policeman Bob Davis had to deal with these clubs as part of
his daily routine. 'They caused real disturbances, because there
were fights and God knows what going on till four or five in
the morning, until we eventually got to grips with them. And I
mean *big* trouble, not minor things. The crime we had around
here then was a lot more violent than today; there were a
lot more serious assaults: people with their legs shot off with
shotguns and axes in their heads and this kind of thing. Night
after night after night.'[82]

By 1958 the British economy had fallen into a slight depression,
provoked largely by Suez and the Government's attempts to
control inflation. Unemployment was approaching half a million
– 2.2 per cent of the total population – and notices of redundancy
were being announced with worrying frequency. [83] The most
soothing comment that the Government made on unemployment in 1958 was that 'no one should be surprised or shocked
if it proves necessary that it should go somewhat further'.[84]

This did little to calm unease about the future, reflected
in the increasingly shrill calls for immigration control. James

Lindsay (Conservative, Devon), an ex-Etonian and landowner in South Africa, asked the House of Commons in April 1958 whether, in the light of rising unemployment, it was not right to act now to curb the influx of West Indian labour. Lindsay was concerned that unemployment would be aggravated by the 'flood of immigrants'. He urged Honourable Members to question closely any decision to increase the supply of unskilled labour at a time when there was likely to be a decrease in demand. Lindsay also warned that Britain could be in danger of 'starting on the road of becoming a multi-racial society', and expressed anxiety about the tendency of West Indians to 'separate themselves off into certain jobs and housing districts' which he thought a 'deplorable and very disturbing element'. Above all, he warned that unless the Government acted soon to stem the flow of black people, white people might be forced to take the law into their own hands:

> There is always the possibility of trouble, and it is the risk of trouble, the threat, which is so important. Unless there are overwhelming advantages – and I cannot see them – we ought not to lay ourselves open to this possible trouble.

Controversial statements such as these were unlikely to allay burgeoning racial fears. At the end of his Commons speech, which he delivered only four months before the Notting Hill riots, Lindsay said he welcomed the debate on the 'colour problem' and hoped it would be 'carried on in the country'.[85]

At the same time, the press stepped up its vitriol against the West Indians, plumbing new depths. The Sunday paper, *The People* splashed the headline '*For Their Own Sakes Stop Them Now*' across its centre pages in May.

> With the greatest possible urgency the *People* now asks the government to put up a bar against the free admission of coloured immigrants to Britain. We are not yielding to colour prejudice. But the wave of immigrants rolling all over our shores has now risen to threatening proportions.[86]

The article went on to ask what would happen to those hundreds of West Indians who, because the boom had ended, were virtually unemployable in Britain? 'These people came here as citizens of a free and equal commonwealth, to improve their lot. Through no fault of their own they have failed. So they cannot be dealt with harshly. They should, gently but firmly, be made to go.'[87]

Newspapers were one vehicle for spreading anti-black sentiments among white working-class communities. Another were the extreme racist groups which homed in on Notting Hill in the months leading up to the riots, recognising that as a closed community, hostile towards outsiders, the Dale would make fertile ground for their views. Indeed, Notting Dale became one of the centres of the post-war fascist revival. A number of small splinter parties actively agitated within the white community, calling for the repatriation of West Indians. Among their numbers were leading figures on the extreme right – Colin Jordan, John Bean and John Tyndall.[88]

Colin Jordan's group, the White Defence League, had its headquarters in Notting Hill out of which they played martial music at high volume. A large swastika hung from a mast on top of the building.[89] Jordan published his own broadsheet, *Black and White News*, which claimed to 'expose' the inherent inferiority of black people. A group slightly more on the side-lines was the League of Empire Loyalists, founded by A.K. Chesterton in 1954. It cultivated a respectable façade, flirting with right-wing Conservative MPs and by 1958 it had won a following of over 3,000. The League stood for the struggle to preserve traditional British values and the Empire against black immigration and the 'Jewish plot for world domination'. The third group was John Bean's National Labour Party, which circulated a leaflet called *COMBAT* around Notting Hill just before the riots. It still lingered on the theme of the 'Judaeo-Communist-Masonic plot', asking whether Hitler was really our enemy, but the target of its invective had shifted from the 'Jewish Red Peril' to the new 'Coloured Peril':

> Coloured immigration must be stopped. Not only does it aggravate the housing problem and constitute a serious threat to workers' living standards in view of increasing unemployment, but most importantly, it will turn our nation into a race of mongrels.[90]

All these organisations were allowed to openly tout their opinions without fear of legal reprisal. This was due partly to the failure of the authorities to take their activities seriously, and partly to the inherent weakness of the law as it stood in the 1950s. The offence of defamation could only be invoked to protect individuals, not groups. This gave the fascists legal sanction to openly abuse black people vocally or on the printed page. The only way that they could be prosecuted was if they were accused of intending to provoke a breach of the peace, a charge notoriously difficult to prove.[91]

The fascist groups did not so much create racial hatred, as exploit and encourage it. John Garrett, who as a teenager was involved in the riots, says that prejudice was already well established in the area before the fascists started leafletting.[92] The importance of their presence in Notting Dale was that they fomented and intensified racial hatred, playing on the fears of the white community. By providing an organised forum and by urging white people to take action, the fascists helped to translate racial hatred from its passive to its active voice – from pub gossip to street violence.

The fascists made their entry into the white community largely through pubs. George Clark remembers that there were three pubs in Notting Hill where the fascists used to operate. They would ingratiate themselves with local people prior to meetings by buying rounds of drinks, which tended to win trust, and then use pub gossip to disseminate the most virulent racism.[93]

The biggest and most influential fascist party during the 1950s was Oswald Mosley's Union Movement, the post-war version of his British Union of Fascists that had spearheaded the attack on Jews in London's East End in the 1930s. By the 1950s Mosley was, on a national level, a defeated man. Imprisoned during the war for supporting Hitler, he had lost most of his following and in 1951 he went to live abroad. But five years later he was back, leading the Union Movement against a new target – black people. At the time of the riots, the Union Movement was at its peak, with a membership of 1,500.

Mosley veiled his extreme views with a paper-thin pseudo-liberal veneer. 'We don't want a colour bar – of any sort!' claimed his paper, *Action*, in May 1958. 'We want an end to the thing which causes the colour bar: the immigration of thousands of completely different people who take our homes and threaten our jobs.'[94] A range of arguments were exploited in the Union Movement's campaigns, from sensationalist claims that blacks were spreading vice and disease, to the suggestion that it was in their own interests to be kept out of Britain. Mosley wanted all black immigrants repatriated, their boat fares to be paid by the Government. Britain should also sponsor development programmes in the Caribbean to reduce the economic need of emigration from the West Indies. The striking point about all these arguments is that, apart from Mosley's desire to repatriate all blacks, they were remarkably similar to demands for immigration control being raised by 'respectable' bodies such as the press and Government. For instance, while Mosley was busily campaigning in Notting Hill, the Colonial Office was holding confidential discussions on 'the development of resources in the West Indies as a means to reducing immigration into the United Kingdom'.[95]

Notting Hill held pride of place in the Union Movement's campaign to stir up racial unrest. In 1956, Mosley made his first public speech after his return from the political wilderness in Kensington town hall, speaking to a crowd of 600. From January 1958, the Union Movement held regular meetings on the street corners of Notting Hill, which were well-attended, particularly by young white men. As the year progressed the fascists clearly felt that they were making some headway among poor white communities such as Notting Dale. On 8 August, less than one month before race riots broke out, *Action* made an accurate prediction. 'Times have changed. The people are waking up. Once again our critics can't take it. But stick close, boys, and hang on tight. There's a lot more coming.'[96]

After London, one of the largest West Indian communities in the 1950s was to be found in Nottingham, with a black population in 1958 of around 3,000 out of a total of 350,000.[97] One area of West Indian settlement was St Ann's, near the city centre, which had its own West Indian grocers, barbers and a West Indian club where they held weekly dances, sporting events and political meetings.

The houses in St Ann's were two-storey tenements, rising steeply on either side of a valley, divided by the main thoroughfare and shopping centre – St Ann's Well Road. They were plain-fronted buildings, stained dark with soot, with their front doors opening directly into the ground-floor parlour and kitchen.

In the backyards were brick sheds for toilets and the occasional coal-cellar. Separating the back-to-backs were thin alleyways, which served as playgrounds for children and meeting places for adults. Many of the cobbled streets were still gas-lit in the fifties. The only tree-lined street was Robin Hood Chase, a promenade popular with courting couples, which wound its way up one side of the valley. Apart from the Chase, St Ann's was an unbroken mass of uniform houses. From a distance all that could be seen were tightly packed rows of chimneys, like soldiers in a military parade – Nottingham's equivalent of Coronation Street.[98]

The area had been developed in the 1880s to house Irish, Scots, Welsh and English migrants who came to Nottingham from all over, attracted by the boom in its textile industry. The transient and migratory nature of the population of St Ann's continued into the 1950s which, like the Colville area in Notting Hill, made it more accessible to black people than any other part of Nottingham. St Ann's had a large Polish community and Eastern European and Asian landlords living in the area were generally more willing to rent rooms to the West Indians than local English residents.[99]

It was a wretched part of the city. The houses in St Ann's had been built in the late nineteenth century out of a soft brick which was crumbling by the 1950s. Drainage pipes were made from the same material and in winter they would crack, forming open sewers. Hardly any of the houses had baths, and although accommodation was not in such short supply as in London, the area was very overcrowded. The population density of St Ann's in 1961 was 62.4 persons per acre, compared with 17 in Nottingham as a whole.[100] St Ann's was like Notting Dale and the Colville area combined. It had an insular white working-class community like Notting Dale, fond of drinking with over 70 pubs in a one-mile radius.[101] And it also had many of the same characteristics as the Colville area's West Indian community – Shebeens, cafés, West Indian shops and barbers.

Although there is no evidence of fascist activity in St Ann's, relations between white and black residents had become markedly strained by the beginning of 1958. Black people complained that they were being abused in the streets, and that the police were doing nothing to protect them. In the middle of August a gang of twenty white youths chased a West Indian, Alphonso

Walton, along St Ann's Well Road, and kicked him while he was on the ground for over ten minutes.[102]

Gradually, incidents like this began to escalate and an electric tension gripped the neighbourhood. White men, always in groups, attacked individual West Indians in the dimly lit maze of back-alleys which provided the perfect terrain for ambushes. Late one night the Jamaican Samuel Roberts was walking home to his rented room in St Ann's after a shift on the buses. He saw a group of white men coming towards him, and having been warned that such groups spelt danger, he took to his heels. He was caught just as he reached his front door, and put in hospital for over a week. [103]

There is a long history of racial violence of this sort in England. Irish people were popular objects of harassment earlier in the century, as were the Jews. Germans and Austrians in the First World War and Italians and Germans in the Second World War were branded as spies and brutally treated by individuals and the authorities.[104] For black people, racial attacks go back at least as far as 1919 when large crowds of whites gathered in Cardiff after a black man was alleged to have made an offensive remark to a white woman. In the ensuing fighting three people died.[105] In August 1948 a crowd of 2,000 whites attacked black seamen in Liverpool after the latter had protested against the National Union of Seamen's efforts to keep them off British ships.[106] In 1954 West Indians living in Camden Town, London, were attacked for two days running and one of their houses set on fire with petrol bombs.[107]

In Notting Hill, Irish people had been harassed back in the 1860s, through a combination of racial animosity and religious spite. 'Who are you for, the Pope or Garibaldi' was the favourite challenge. A serious riot even broke out which took 300 policemen to control.[108] During the Second World War Italian stall-holders in Portobello Road were picked on and forced to pack up and leave, though some more fortunate Italians avoided harassment by changing their names.[109]

1958 was one of those freak years when England actually enjoyed a summer. From June to late September the country was bathed in hot sunshine, which drew people out of their houses to go sunbathing in the parks, or just to bask on their front doorsteps. In the long evenings people would stroll in the streets, drink outside pubs, or sit at opened windows. It was a peculiarly happy setting for the unhappy events that were to follow.

Pansy Jeffrey first came to Britain in the late 1940s to study, but went back to British Guiana a few years later. In 1956 she returned to Britain and went to live in Notting Hill. She was struck at once by a change in atmosphere. She remembers that on her first visit black students were treated with some respect: 'They felt that as students we would not settle but go back, so it wasn't a problem. There was beautiful kindness.' But in 1956 that kindness had turned sour: 'I was coming back not as a student but as a grown up – looking for a job. Well, that was a bit different. . . And England had changed completely because the tolerance had gone and there was the beginning of anger.'[110]

Isolated attacks against black people began to occur in Notting Hill from July. At first the attacks were skirmishes rather than really serious assaults, and West Indians comforted themselves with the thought that they amounted to nothing more than a couple of lads letting off steam: 'They were kind of *gentle* attacks,' says Ivo de Souza. 'People weren't coming at us with knives at the start; it began with verbal abuse, and perhaps a few sticks and stones.'[111] One popular form of harassment was to stop black people in the street and ask them for a cigarette. The West Indians could either offer one and be humiliated by losing the whole packet, or refuse and suffer the brutal consequences. As these attacks become more common and less gentle, black people started moving about in groups and avoided the most dangerous areas, especially Notting Dale. A group of Ivo de Souza's friends were walking just off Ladbroke Grove on their way to his house for dinner and as they turned a corner they noticed twenty white men watching them across the street. Someone said that they looked very unfriendly and it was best to get out as quickly as possible; others were more brash and refused to be intimidated. Suddenly a shower of stones descended upon them and they had to run down the street to the nearest station.[112]

The violence was becoming noticeably more regular and more organised. White residents set up a vigilante squad supposedly to clear the streets of vice and prostitution. They called for powers to deport black people convicted of sexual offences and threatened to take action themselves if government didn't move fast.[113] Then, on 14th July a café in Shepherds Bush owned by a West Indian was attacked by fifteen white men armed with sticks. They descended on the café in cars and on foot and proceeded to demolish it, quite methodically, beginning with the chairs, then the tables and finally the plates and cups. The owner, Samuel Thomas, said that it was all over in five minutes. 'It was like an earthquake. I didn't try and stop them because I would have been killed.'[114] Five white men were arrested and charged, among them a 17-year-old from Wilsham Street in the heart of Notting Dale. The magistrate hearing the case, E.R. Guest, was astonished that the police did not oppose bail. 'For some reason,' he said, 'the smallest dishonesty is met with the greatest possible care, but in these cases, which are far more serious, everybody says lightly, "Oh! let them go. Never mind bail. Never mind the public." I am always pointing out here that violence in the street is the gravest thing this court has to deal with.'[115]

In the first week of August a West Indian, Charles Appio, was assaulted in Ladbroke Grove. He was walking towards the tube when he had to step aside to let a group of white youths pass. One of them barged into him. He walked on, but as he was just entering the station one of the white men grabbed him from the back, spun him round and punched him full in the face. As he sank to his knees he was hit repeatedly. 'Why are you doing this?' he managed to ask in between blows.[116] When three of the white men appeared in court, again in front of Guest, the magistrate was astounded that the police had made no arrangements for prosecution. 'Why the prosecution is not represented in these matters which are a test of civilisation I do not know. Whether or not people walk safely in the streets distinguishes civilisation from the lack of it. Nobody looks upon it as a matter of the slightest importance.'[117]

As August passed, the attacks intensified in scale and severity. On 17th August two houses occupied by West Indians were pelted with bottles and bricks by a group of whites. Seven black men retaliated and one of the whites was stabbed in the back.[118] Fascist agitation also reached a new pitch.

Five days before serious rioting erupted in Notting Hill and Nottingham, the editor of a London-based black newspaper, *The West Indian Gazette*, received a threatening letter from the 'Ku-Klux-Klan'. 'My Dear Mr B. Ape,' it said. 'We, the Aryan Knights miss nothing. Close attention has been paid to every issue of this rag, and I do sincerely assure you, the information gleaned has proven of great value to the Klan.'[119]

On 11th August a West Indian was set upon in Notting Hill and windows of nearby shops smashed. Three days later a West African student was chased in a Notting Dale side-street, narrowly escaping by hiding in a bush. On the 15th a local paper carried the headline '*Violence wave scares Ladbroke Grove area*', and described racial hostility as a 'serious and growing problem'. Local residents, who asked not to be named for fear of reprisals, were reported as saying 'The situation could easily lead to violence of the worst kind' and 'This is only the beginning; unless something drastic is done soon I don't know what the consequences will be'.[120] In desperation, a petition was organised calling for urgent action to stem the escalating violence.

But the situation continued to deteriorate without so much as a statement of reassurance from the police or one extra constable being put on the beat. Groups of white men roamed freely as though they had been granted total immunity from the law. As the month neared its end E.R. Guest made one last plea for help: 'It is a matter of considerable public importance that something should be done seriously to stop street disorders in North Kensington. They are not only a disgrace to the neighbourhood but also extremely dangerous for ordinary decent citizens.'[121]

But one magistrate cannot hold back a storm. In any case, his cry for help came too late: the first major incidents of racial violence both in Nottingham and London broke out the next day.

7
Riot

It all started one Saturday night, 23rd August 1958, in the Chase Tavern in Nottingham, one of the only pubs in St Ann's where West Indians could drink. A Jamaican man was talking to a white woman next to the bar. This was clearly an impropriety in the eyes of a white man standing close by who shouted 'Lay off that woman'. The Jamaican did not take kindly to this suggestion. Over the weeks and months disappointment – at being turned away from jobs, houses, public places – had turned to resentment and resentment to bitterness. He had had enough.[1]

Who punched whom first is not known. But a scuffle ensued, provoking other scuffles which in turn broke into a larger fight, spilling out of the pub onto the St Ann's Well Road. Black men withdrew into small groups, outnumbered by the crowd of whites which grew steadily as people poured out of the Tavern and neighbouring houses. Some were just curious to find out what was going on; others were eager to join the affray. 'Go home to your own country' they jeered, brandishing an improvised armoury of broken bottles, knives, razors and stakes. Black people were set upon and attacked; others ran to their homes. Samuel Roberts, who had only recently been beaten up outside his house in St Ann's, has the events of that night etched into his memory. 'The white people were screaming and shouting they were going to kill niggers, just like they talk about hunting badgers in the wood. They were trying to drive us out. In the pub they said "Let's go hunt the niggers" and then they went out for the kill.'[2]

The West Indians in St Ann's were used to isolated racial attacks of the sort that had been mounting through the summer. But the large baying crowd that now faced and threatened to kill them was qualitatively different from anything they had experienced before. By this stage the West Indians had lost almost all trust in the ability or inclination of the police to protect them.[3] Many black people decided to keep out of the way of the crowd and stay indoors. But some younger blacks retaliated, arming themselves with anything they could lay their hands on – bricks, stones, sticks. Some had knives and used them.

What had begun as a pub brawl turned suddenly into a major race riot. West Indians were ambushed down back-alleys and severely beaten and other black men jumped into cars and drove at high speeds at the crowd.[4] According to Nottingham's police chief Athelstan Popkess the crowd consisted almost entirely of whites hostile towards blacks. All the serious injuries, he said, were inflicted within a matter of seconds before the arrival of the police, the offenders absconding immediately up dark alleyways and by-streets.[5] This was somewhat misleading, however, as it took the police so long to arrive at the scene of the fighting that the white crowd had already grown to over 1,000 strong. Pitched battles between whites and blacks were raging fiercely, and they continued for a total of ninety minutes. Eight people, black and white, were hospitalised, two with stab wounds to the back. A white man was seriously injured and had to have thirty-seven stitches sewn across his throat. His distraught wife told reporters how she had found him at the side of the road with his throat cut. 'He was bleeding from ear to ear,' she said.[6]

The West Indians who fought were all men – the women took shelter in their homes. But some white women were involved in the predominantly male crowd of attackers. A woman in her late forties, Abigail Blagdon, launched into a small group of West Indians huddled round a motor-cycle. She stormed straight at them brandishing a heavy walking stick and threatening to nobble the first one that made the wrong move.[7]

Other white women were terrified by the fighting. Their fear of black men was so intense that the sight of West Indians fighting was like living through a hideous nightmare haunted by primitive monsters. 'I have never seen anything like it in my life,' said Mrs Byatt. 'There was blood everywhere. The darkies were going for anyone in sight. The assaults were not the work of humans.'[8] Another woman said: 'The men who attacked us were all young coloured chaps. They had all been drinking and we were frightened to death to walk anywhere near them. We want a curfew imposed on them.'[9]

Fighting carried on late into Saturday night until Chief Constable Popkess' men, with Alsatian dogs and Black Marias, finally managed to disperse the crowd. White people began to drift back to their crumbling tenements while black people, their curtains drawn, stayed indoors wondering what would happen next. Apart from fear, the sense of isolation must have been extreme: cut off as they were, trapped and under siege. If any of the West Indians had any lingering doubts about their status within St Ann's, the Chase Tavern – the one place where they could mingle freely and feel a part of the community – announced the next day that it was closing its doors to them. The licensee, Fred Alsopp, blamed black people for the disturbances. 'I have had a lot of trouble recently and I have had to bar some of the "bad boys". I was never a colour bar person until I took over this house ten weeks ago. But, oh boy! What a lot of trouble the coloured men can cause.'[10]

Some West Indians were more deeply shocked than others. John Wray arrived in Nottingham from Jamaica only three months before the riots erupted. 'I felt I was coming to *improve* myself,' he says, 'to climb up to a higher dimension. And then the next thing I knew I was being shouted at by white people as they passed my window. Dirty, racist, taunting remarks.'[11] The day after the fighting, Wray was bemused. He could not tell what white people were thinking. 'Everybody kept very quiet and still, clammed up.'[12]

The next night, Sunday, crowds appeared again on the streets of St Ann's, but this time the police were out in force and quickly dispersed groups as soon as they formed. By Monday morning normality appeared to have returned. In the dim red-brick side-streets, whites and blacks stood around

in separate groups discussing the previous night's disorders in
a disconnected way. Black people looked nervous and dazed.
Already those most downcast were talking about accepting the
last humiliation and getting a ship home.[13]

On that same Saturday night, 23rd August, while the
Nottingham disturbances were just beginning, a group of nine
white youths crammed themselves into a car and set out on a
pleasure tour of west London which was to end with three black
men in hospital for several weeks and the nine youths locked
up in prison for four years. Having been drinking in a pub
named, ironically enough, the 'General Smuts'[14] they cruised
around Shepherds Bush and Notting Hill, 'nigger hunting'. All
of them teenagers, they came from Hammersmith, Acton, and
White City; one lived in Hunt Street in the heart of Notting
Dale.[15] Why they acted as they did that night remains obscure.
The leader of the Rugby club in Notting Dale, where they were
regular members, thought perhaps it was because the youth
club was closed. Being at a loose end the idea occurred to them to
have a go at black people instead. 'Those sorts of boys take up
any activity to break the boredom,' he said.[16] Only one of the
youths objected to the expedition – the owner of the car, who
thought that nine people would be too much of a squeeze.

They set out in the small hours, the boot of the car full of
home-made weapons: a starting handle, an air pistol, table legs,
chains, iron-railings with spear-shaped ends and four blocks of
wood.[17] Spotting the first solitary West Indian in a deserted
street they pulled over and got out. The West Indian quickly
understood what was coming, and sped down the street, but
not fast enough – he was caught and smashed over the head
with an iron bar. The boys calmly got back into the car and set
off again. Between three and five o'clock in the morning they
made a further three attacks – in Shepherds Bush, in Wood
Lane and the third in Notting Hill. Never attacking groups of
blacks, the largest number of West Indians they picked on was
two. Five West Indians were seriously injured. Later, when
the nine youths were hauled in front of the courts, one of the
West Indians, Mathew Lucien, had to be pushed into court in
a wheelchair. The magistrate, E.R. Guest, was appalled when
he saw another, John Pirmal, being brought in on a stretcher,

suffering from a half-inch wound to the chest. He said that if
there was ever a case in which it would be contrary to the public
interest to grant bail, it was this, adding that he had 'never seen
a man brought into court in such a state. I don't think he is
fit to give evidence.'[18]

The Nottingham race riots and the attacks in west London
hit the newspaper headlines on the Monday morning[19] and
the country waited with bated breath to see what would
happen next. The hot, sticky London air was pregnant with
further unrest. But during the following week the tension
remained unbroken.[20] Just when concerned observers were
beginning to feel optimistic that the unrest would turn out to
be no more than passing incidents, two Nottingham MPs, one
Conservative, the other Labour, publicly called for an end to the
uncontrolled entry of black people into Britain. On Tuesday 26th
August, two days after the riots in St Ann's, James Harrison
(Labour, Nottingham North) said that the 'open door' policy
was completely impractical under modern conditions. 'Some
of my parliamentary colleagues and I suggested in 1947 that
this policy should be seriously examined – only to be accused
of colour prejudice.' He felt that the keen competition for
housing and the 'ominous' unemployment that black people
were now facing, were problems which could only be dealt with
at government level.[21]

The Conservative Member for Nottingham Central, J.K.
Cordeaux, travelled to London with the express purpose of
informing Cabinet Ministers that he had been convinced by
the race riots that black immigration should be curtailed: 'I
have believed for some time,' he said, 'that there ought to
be a quota or definite restrictions on people coming into this
country from overseas. I have been worried about this matter
because I feared that something serious like this might occur.
What has happened emphasises the seriousness of the position
and the urgency of the matter. I want to put this before
the Minister.'[22]

While in London, Cordeaux appeared on BBC's *Tonight*
programme, in conversation with journalist James Cameron.
'The problem is of British law and order, British education,
and it is one for us to solve. The coloured man cannot be

blamed whatever his behaviour,' said Cameron. But Cordeaux
twisted this argument. 'I agree,' he replied. 'No blame attaches
to the immigrants – it attaches to our Government for allowing
unrestricted immigration.'[23]

West Indians in St Ann's were dismayed by the MPs'
statements, fearing they would provoke further violence. They
accused Harrison of taking sides and Cordeaux of leaving
Nottingham instead of staying and appealing for calm and
restraint.[24] In these heady days the West Indians felt as if they
were under attack from all sides, for even those who purported
to be their friends supplied their enemies with ammunition.
Just after the first rioting a local cleric – the Reverend C.W.
Harrington, Vicar of Woodborough and a former minister in the
Orange Free State, South Africa – said that he was opposed to
any form of racial discrimination having seen the consequences
of apartheid. But he accepted that immigration control was
necessary because Britain was 'overcrowded', although this
should be on educational rather than racial grounds. 'Black
people are human beings. They are not animals, although they
sometimes behave like it because they have not our cultural or
educational background.'[25]

Meanwhile, politicians and pressmen were busily competing
among themselves to predict where the next round of 'nigger
bashing' would rear its head. As if placing bets, newspapers ran
lists of the most likely trouble spots. Those multi-racial areas
regarded as long-shots were Birmingham's Handsworth and
Moss Side in Manchester, where relations between whites and
blacks were said to be cordial. Hammersmith was recommended
as a safer bet, because gangs of Teddy Boys had been seen
cruising the streets on weekend evenings looking for Africans
or West Indians. They chose streets where only the occasional
black person was to be found and then attacked in a ratio of
half-a-dozen to one. Brixton was also a front runner, owing to
the activity of fascists who were distributing leaflets under the
title: 'members of the Brixton branch of the Ku-Klux-Klan'.[26]

But odds on favourite in everybody's book was Notting Hill.
By the last week of August even the national papers were
warning that west London was showing all the signs of being
a potential trouble area. The *Manchester Guardian* said on 27th
August that Notting Hill had been unsettled for the previous

three weeks, with regular fights and attempts to run down black pedestrians with cars on Saturday nights.[27] Despite such clear omens the local Notting Hill police still did not place any extra bobbies on the beat.

In contrast, the police were already on guard in St Ann's, Nottingham, when crowds of white people gathered on the night of Saturday 30th August, exactly one week after the first riots. There was hardly a black person in sight, the West Indians having decided that the only form of protection was to hide. This strategy proved successful in that very few black people were attacked that night. Chief Constable Athelstan Popkess paid tribute to the black community: 'The coloured people behaved in an exemplary way by keeping out of the way. Indeed, they were an example to some of our rougher elements. The people primarily concerned were irresponsible Teddy Boys and persons who had had a lot to drink.'[28] But three black people thought it safe to drive through the area. As their car passed the Chase Tavern they were suddenly pounced on by a crowd of hundreds of whites who tried to overturn the car, screaming 'Let's lynch the niggers!' The West Indians were lucky to escape with their lives. Just in time, the police managed to force their way through the crowd and, reaching the car, told them to 'Go like hell!' which they accordingly did.[29]

With no other black people around to bait, the crowd, reportedly over 4,000 strong by the end of the evening,[30] turned against itself. Fighting broke out between different groups of white men, the biggest incident being provoked by a television reporter who orchestrated a mock scuffle for the benefit of the cameras. The bright flash of his magnesium flare, illuminating what seemed to be a real-life battle, created pandemonium. Police reinforcements were attacked as they came in from side alleys, and fierce fighting ensued.

Twenty-four people – all white – were arrested and charged under the Public Order Act. Three men were given custodial sentences of three months for obstructing the police, and another fifteen were fined between £10 and £30. These were relatively minor penalties for major rioting, although friends and relatives of the accused appeared to think otherwise. As the sentences were read out in Nottingham magistrates court, uproar broke out from the public benches. Men and women shouted at the judge 'You're all for the niggers!' Several people were evicted, one woman fainted and had to be carried out and it took four police officers to drag another woman, screaming in protest at the sentences, from the courtroom.[31]

As Nottingham was experiencing its second weekend of rioting, west London erupted. The first incident occurred on Friday evening when Majbritt Morrison, a Swedish woman, was arguing with her Jamaican husband Raymond outside Latimer Road tube station in Notting Dale. Noticing the row, curious white people began to gather round. Men started shouting at Raymond, thinking it was their duty to protect a white woman from a black man. This display of chivalry failed to impress Majbritt Morrison, however, who added fuel to the fire by trying to protect her husband. In the eyes of the white men she had committed the ultimate sin by turning her back on her own race.[32]

Just as the argument began to turn ugly, a group of the Morrisons' West Indian friends stepped into the dispute. A fight broke out which was resolved without serious injuries. But that was just the beginning. Word began to spread around the Dale that it was time to teach the 'niggers' and their 'white trash' a lesson. Next night the pubs were packed and bristling with anti-black sentiment. As the drink flowed, and people's tongues loosened, racial hatred reached fever pitch. Instead of going home at closing time, men stood around in crowds outside the pubs in Bramley Road, looking restive and aggressive.

Suddenly, Majbritt Morrison was spotted walking towards them. She was jeered and jostled: 'Nigger lover! Kill her!' She continued to walk straight ahead and was bruised by milk bottles before reaching home, where she found the police already waiting for her. They told her to go inside, and when she persistently refused she was arrested, charged with obstructing the police and taken to Notting Hill police station where she was held until 5 a.m.[33]

After she had been taken away, the crowd went on the rampage. Windows in Blechynden Street, off Bramley Road, were systematically smashed and the police arrived just in time to prevent the crowd attacking a party being held by

King Dick. Opting for the easiest means of defusing the crisis, the police carved a passage through the crowd and escorted the West Indians out of Notting Dale.[34] This certainly averted a potentially disastrous confrontation by removing the object of the crowd's aggression. But it did little to avert further rioting, for in the eyes of the white rioters these tactics seemed to confirm their belief that through violence they could drive black people out of Notting Dale.

Early in the evening of the following day, Sunday 31st August, a gang of around 100 white teenagers, armed with sticks, iron bars and knives, gathered under the railway arches outside Latimer Road station. Slowly the crowd began to swell, until by 8.00 pm 400 people were reported milling around the streets, shouting 'We'll kill the black bastards!' 'Why don't you send them home?' A group of black people were set upon and a woman stabbed in the shoulder. A man was slashed across the neck and taken to hospital, and a ten-year-old boy, who had got caught up in the affray, was hit in the mouth with a broken bottle.[35]

Black people living in Notting Dale and the neighbouring Colville area were astonished by the fighting. 'It was totally unexpected,' says Baron Baker. 'I'd never seen such strange behaviour in my life. White people getting up in hysteria, saying "Let's lynch the niggers!" "Let's burn their homes!" '[36] Until the weekend of the riots, black people had been accustomed to walk in groups at night, to protect themselves against attack. Now even that was insufficient safeguard against the hordes of hostile whites. So they stayed indoors, in the hope that eventually the crowds would fade away.[37]

Robbed of their prey, the white teenagers turned against the police. On the Sunday night there were still only ten constables on the beat in Notting Hill. They were caught totally off balance when they suddenly found themselves confronted by crowds of more than 400 white rioters, spitting at them and shouting 'You coppers are all for the niggers!' 'Why do you coppers only pinch white blokes?' 'Coppers are nigger lovers!'[38]

Four officers on the beat in Bramley Road, Notting Dale, were attacked. One was knocked to the ground, surrounded and kicked in the face, and a second was cut in the face with bits of glass when a flying bottle smashed against his police car. In another side-street three officers were pinned against a wall and pelted with stones and bottles.[39] The fighting, against black people and then against the police, ran sporadically for four hours until midnight when the crowds began to thin and only the die-hards were left hanging around the Dale, shouting obscenities into the dark.

On Monday, 1st September, Notting Hill experienced some of the worst rioting that Britain has seen this century. Already by the afternoon it was gripped by an unhealthy mood and a tense atmosphere hung over the Colville area and Notting Dale. Only a handful of black faces were to be seen outdoors and white people looked preoccupied and tense. But apart from these danger signals it was business as usual. Shops were open, the buses were running and although the odd police car lurked at a junction, it all seemed too calm, if anything, for comfort.

In the late afternoon the streets began to fill once again with roving gangs. In an attempt to pacify the crowds the local Labour MP, George Rogers, toured the area in a loud-speaker van appealing for 'common sense, decency and tolerance',[40] but to little avail. That afternoon a young African student, Seymour Manning, came down from Derby to visit a friend in Notting Dale. He must have been unaware of the rioting, for he walked out of Latimer Road station into Notting Dale with a firm, confident stride, as if nothing was untoward. As he turned into Bramley Road he was greeted by a wall of screams and jeers coming from a large group of white people blocking the road. Manning froze, then spun on his heels and sprinted back towards the Underground, his tie and college blazer streaming out behind him. The gang caught up with him and he was thrown to the ground, kicked and his leg twisted. Somehow he managed to wriggle loose and again he ran for his life. Just as his pursuers closed in for a second time, he flung himself into a greengrocer's shop and slammed the door behind him.[41]

Manning escaped by the skin of his teeth. Not only had he reached the greengrocer's with seconds to spare, but he was also fortunate that the shopkeeper had no time for the rioters. She bolted the door against the crowd which was now over 200 strong and swarming outside shouting 'Lynch him!' It took

police on horseback and in radio squad cars, and twenty constables on foot, half an hour to disperse the crowd before they
could rescue Manning and escort him to safety.

A reporter asked young white men outside the shop why they
wanted to lynch the African student. A teenager said: 'Just tell
your readers we've got a bad enough housing shortage around
here without them moving in. Keep Britain White.' One of the
men who caught Manning before he reached the safety of the
greengrocer's said: 'I half twisted his leg off anyway. We'd have
tore him apart if it hadn't been for the police.' He called himself
local and insisted that the Notting Hill boys could handle 'their
own problem'. But he also claimed he had mates from the
Elephant and Castle who were coming over 'to help us finish
the job'. They planned a paraffin raid on some second-storey flats
where white girls were living with West Indians. 'Come back
tomorrow night, mister, for the next instalment,' he said.[42]

Although there is no evidence on which one could base an
accurate estimate, it appears that the rioters were acting with
the blessing of the majority of Notting Dale's white community.
The West Indians certainly believed that to be the case. Baron
Baker remembers feeling that every white person was against
him: 'It was not only just simple young chaps, or just one section
of the people. It was the entire community that was up against
us.'[43] White people from Notting Dale who tried to stop the
carnage were treated severely by their own people. Jean Maggs
remembers that one of her friends helped a black man who had
been badly cut and was lying bleeding on the pavement. She
called an ambulance and dressed his wounds with pieces of
material torn from her clothing. When her brother found out
about this he refused to speak to her for six months.[44]

The vast majority of white people living in and around the
riot area maintained a complicit silence. Chris Lemaitre from
Trinidad remembers with bitterness how little protection was
offered black people by local publicans. During the riots he
was drinking in a pub in North Kensington with some other
West Indians when suddenly they were attacked by a group
of whites. The owner refused to call the police and instead
expelled Lemaitre and his friends from the pub.[45] There were
a few examples of white people coming to the assistance of
their black neighbours. Members of the local Communist Party

ferried black people out of the trouble spots, but this was the
exception to the rule. Colin MacInnes was shocked that, apart
from the greengrocer who protected Manning, white people
remained passive in the face of the riots:

> What I'd just seen made me feel weak and hopeless: most of all
> because except for that old vegetable woman no one, absolutely
> no one, had reacted against this thing. You looked around to find
> members of the other team – even just a few of us – and there
> weren't any.[46]

Later that Monday night the fascists made their greatest
impact. From the start of the riots the fascist groups were
quick to make their presence felt. A few days after the first
Nottingham fights, a woman who had been quoted in the
newspapers saying it was time to stem the flow of blacks
received a letter posted from west London and attributed to
the Ku-Klux-Klan, urging her to set up a cell in St Ann's.[47] In
Notting Hill fascist broadsheets were distributed in the trouble
spots throughout the riots. The National Labour Party's tract,
Look Out, said: 'A square deal for the negro in his own country.
Has a foreigner taken your job yet? Is a foreigner your
employer? Does a foreigner represent you in Parliament? If not,
then you are fortunate, for your country is steadily being taken
over by the triumphant alien.'[48] A leader of the NLP, John
Steel, was quoted as saying: 'We will be a nation of half-castes.
The result will be that the nation will possess neither the
rhythm of the coloured man, nor the scientific genius of the
European. The only thing we will ever produce is riots, just as
do the mixed races of the world.'[49]

Mosley's Union Movement also circulated a pamphlet in
Notting Hill which advised the white population to 'Take
action now. Protect your jobs. Stop coloured immigration.
Houses for white people – not coloured immigrants.' On
the front of the pamphlet was a cartoon of a black man
wearing a grass skirt and carrying a spear, above the caption:
'People of Kensington act now. Your country is worth fighting
for. Fight with the Union Movement.'[50] Over ten Union
Movement activists leafletted in the centre of the trouble spot,
including Oswald Mosley's son, Alexander. Another activist,
Alexander Marshall, stood outside Ladbroke Grove tube station

provocatively handing leaflets to passing black people; he was arrested and charged with attempting to foment a breach of the peace.[51]

Local pubs provided the fascists with a vital platform. During the riots Notting Dale's pubs were crammed with white people of all ages and both sexes singing 'Old Man River' and 'Bye Bye Blackbird', punctuating the songs with vicious anti-black slogans and chants of 'Keep Britain White'.[52] The fascists attracted even more attention through public rallies. At 8.00 pm on Monday, 1st September, Jeffrey Hamm, Mosley's right-hand man, gave a rousing speech to a crowd of about 700 people in front of Latimer Road station. Hamm was an able orator who knew how to manipulate his audience. He began in measured tones: black people should not be held responsible for the 'colour problem' and violence should be deplored, he said. But gradually, as he began to warm to his subject, his voice grew louder and his invective more extreme. Governments – both Labour and Tory – were the ones to blame, for allowing black people into Britain in the first place. Look what they've done to Notting Hill – they've turned it into a brothel. At the height of his speech Hamm looked as if he were a possessed being, gesticulating wildly in front of a sea of mesmerised up-turned faces, bathed in the yellow glow of the street lamps. Reaching the climax, Hamm shouted 'Get rid of them!' and threw hundreds of leaflets over the excited crowd. A cry exploded as the mob rushed off shouting 'Kill the niggers'. Women grabbed their small children and followed. Dogs ran in among the crowds, barking. Confusion reigned everywhere. Police cars and vans tried to cut off the mob, without success. Within half an hour the crowd, by now over a thousand strong, had broken scores of windows. Women from top floor windows laughed as they called down to the throng 'Go on boys, get yourselves some blacks!'[53]

Until 1st September the disturbances had been geographically circumscribed within Notting Dale. Almost all the rioters were young, working-class men from the immediate neighbourhood and most of the violence occurred within that area. As Peter Taylor, who still works opposite Latimer Road station, put it: 'It started as a purely local thing – all the whites got down on to the street and everybody got stuck in.'[54]

But on the Monday the character of the riots changed. As news of the fighting spread through the media and by word of mouth, people were drawn into Notting Hill. They came from other parts of west London, from south London and even as far away as Reading.[55] The geographical area in which the fighting was located also began to expand. White men from the 'villages' of Notting Dale, the Town, Paddington, Shepherds Bush and Hammersmith began overcoming their traditional hostility and mutual suspicion and started acting collectively. According to John Garrett, who was involved in the riots, the feeling of a common enemy drew them together. Messages would be passed from the Dale to the Town and from there to the Bush. 'Before we'd always been rivals. But during the riots we all got together and became allies.'[56]

Trouble began to spread like a bush fire. Fighting was reported throughout Notting Hill, from Notting Dale in the west to the Colville area in the east. West Indians were attacked even as far out as Shepherds Bush and the Harrow Road. A crowd of 150 white people blocked the tow-path along the canal which forms the northern boundary of Notting Hill and black people were chased and attacked. A house was set ablaze in Paddington by a gang of youths who smashed the front window with stones and threw lighted cloth soaked in paraffin into the living room. The Blue Parrot, a West Indian café in the Harrow Road, was wrecked by 800 bottle-throwing, club-wielding white men and women. It took over thirty policemen with a dozen squad cars and half-a-dozen Black Marias to clear the street. The terrified black people inside the café had been bombarded with over 300 milk bottles and everything in sight was smashed.[57]

Hundreds of outsiders descended on the riot area. The number 28 and 31 buses were full of 'English people coming to see the nigger run'.[58] The Metropolitan line trains were packed full of sightseers pouring into Notting Hill via Latimer Road and Ladbroke Grove stations, as though they were going to a fun-fair, many carrying weapons with very little interference from the police.[59] Some came to ogle and gape, others to participate actively in the fighting. 'Notting Hill does not know what has hit it,' reported the *Manchester Guardian*. 'Among the faces, some of them distorted, some merely curious, that congregate along the pavements there lies an appalling pleasure with self. They are waiting for something to happen, and too many of them will be stirred to gratification when it does.'[60]

And it did. West Indians had to run the gauntlet between rows of white people lining the roads leading from Notting Hill tube station.[61] Small groups of white youths patrolled the streets armed with broken bottles, knives, sticks, chair and table legs, petrol bombs, chains, iron bars and whips. Whites on motor-bikes and cars toured the district looking for black people to beat up, informing each other of the movement of West Indians and where to attack. King Dick, who bears a scar across his forehead where he was struck with a bike chain, remembers witnessing a group of white men attacking a black woman on her own. They casually kicked over the pram she was pushing, throwing her baby onto the pavement.[62] In another incident a 22-year-old slashed a West Indian across the face with a knife. When he was arrested he said to the sergeant 'So a darkie gets chivved. Why all the fuss?'[63]

At the height of the fighting the atmosphere in Notting Hill was one of knife-edge tension. 'You didn't know who you could trust or talk to,' says Ivan Weekes.[64] One of the most extraordinary aspects of the riots was that while they were raging within Notting Hill, outside this small patch of London most people carried on their lives as though nothing was happening. 'Believe me,' wrote Colin MacInnes, 'inside Napoli [Notting Hill] there was blood and thunder but just outside it – only across one single road like some national frontier – you were back in the world of Mrs Dale and What's My Line? and England's Green and Pleasant Land. Napoli was like a prison or concentration camp: inside, blue murder, outside, buses and evening papers and hurrying home to sausages and mash and tea.'[65]

Notting Hill had become a looking-glass world, for all the most mundane objects which everyone takes for granted had suddenly assumed the most profound importance. Milk bottles were turned into missiles, dustbin lids into primitive shields: two symbols of everyday life turned into instruments of destruction.

In 1957 an article by a distinguished Trinidadian journalist, Sir Charles Archibald – 'West Indian window in London' – predicted racial violence and warned the black community

that it would be incapable of defending itself.[66] There was
some truth in that, for the West Indian community in Notting
Hill was indeed unprepared for these mass racial attacks: there
were no sizeable community groups and the only places to meet
were cafés and clubs.

For the first two nights of rioting the West Indians were
dazed and shocked and they stayed indoors in the hope that the
violence would pass. But by the third day, the Monday, it began
to dawn on them that some more drastic form of defence was
required. 'We had to put our foot down,' says Baron Baker. 'Our
homes were being attacked, our women folks were being attacked
and we weren't the ones going out onto the street looking for
trouble. It's only right that one should defend one's home, no
matter who or where you are. We really *had* to fight back,
which we did.'[67] Frances Ezzrecco spearheaded the organisation
of West Indian women: 'If someone comes to hit me, I'm going
to hit back. If I can't hit back with my fists because they're
bigger than me, I'll hit them with anything I can lay my hands
on and that's exactly what happened. We weren't prepared for
that kind of fighting but when it came to it we did it.'[68]

On the Monday West Indians in the Colville area began discussing what action to take. That afternoon they congregated
in the Calypso Club in the centre of the area – Baron Baker,
Frances Ezzrecco, Michael de Freitas, Frank Critchlow and
many others. Michael de Freitas put the issue very bluntly. 'We
don't want committees and representatives,' he said. 'What we
need is to get a few pieces of iron and a bit of organisation so that
tonight when they come in here we can defend ourselves.'[69]

His words struck a chord within the West Indian community.
They gathered an armoury of sticks, knives, meat cleavers and
iron bars which they bought at local ironmongers before the
white shop-keepers realised what was going on. 'Well it was
war, wasn't it?' says King Dick.[70] As night fell they assembled
in Blenheim Crescent, the West Indian men in number nine –
Totobag's café, aptly called 'The Fortress' – and the women in
number six. Three hundred West Indians crammed themselves
into the two houses. The plan was to stay indoors, hidden, and
not move until the white crowd struck, when they were to
use any and every means to repel the attack. King Dick
had spent all afternoon collecting cans of petrol and this

was added with sand to milk bottles to make improvised Molotov cocktails.

As darkness fell the curtains of numbers six and nine Blenheim Crescent were tightly drawn. All the lights were out and not a sound ushered from either house. White crowds, for the third day running, began milling around, looking for black people to attack and, knowing that number nine was a West Indian café, they gathered outside. 'We were all absolutely terrified,' remembers Baron Baker. 'But we had decided to go down fighting. The crowds started to get worked up but they couldn't see us. When they started shouting "Let's burn the niggers out", that's when we hit.'[71]

Up shot the third-floor windows and out flew the Molotov cocktails. Pandemonium ensued as the white crowds scattered, dodging pieces of flying glass, with the West Indians in hot pursuit brandishing knives and choppers. Baron Baker shouted 'Get back to where you come from' – enjoying the irony of the occasion. Only a hard core of white people stayed to confront the West Indians, running between the two houses and hurling missiles back.[72]

This was the turning point. Even those West Indians who had not assembled in Blenheim Crescent began fighting back. A house in Bard Road was attacked by a crowd of over fifty white youths, one of whom hurled a paraffin work-lamp through the ground-floor window onto a bed which caught fire. This time, however, the rioters had bitten off more than they could chew. As people inside wrestled with the flames, the head of the household, a tall black woman, dashed out into the street, wielding a large, glimmering axe. 'I'll murder you for this!' she shouted and the crowd turned back.[73]

At the same time as whites were descending on Notting Hill to join in the affray, black people were doing likewise. Ivan Weekes remembers that Jamaicans showed particular solidarity. 'They were the champions. They came over from Brixton, night by night, to help their brothers in Notting Hill. If they didn't have friends in the area they had relatives. The Jamaicans bore the brunt of the fight in Notting Hill – they fought back fiercely.'[74]

By fighting back the West Indians added a new dimension to the riots, which now threatened to escalate into full-blooded racial war. For the police this was an alarming development, caught as they were between a mass of violent white youths intent on killing 'nigs', and black people determined to defend themselves by any means necessary. By Monday night the police had finally brought reinforcements into Notting Hill from all over London and from other metropolitan forces in one of the largest operations undertaken in the decade. Eleven police cars and several Black Marias were at hand. When the Molotov cocktails started showering down from nine Blenheim Crescent they reacted swiftly. A Black Maria screeched into the road and rammed the front door of the Fortress. Eight West Indians, Baron Baker and Michael de Freitas included, and three whites, were arrested and charged with affray.[75]

The next day, Tuesday 2nd September, Notting Hill looked like a scene from a film set in the American South. People stood about in the heat outside their doors, leaned on balconies, or sat sweating behind the blistered window-sills of Rachman's properties. Policemen walked about, trying to look casual, and Black Marias were positioned at intersections.[76] As it began to get dark gangs of several hundred youths started roaming around the Colville area shouting: 'We want a nigger.' Police vans rounded on gangs of whites in Notting Hill and Paddington and forty-nine people were arrested.

It was on this fourth night of rioting that the police, who had until then been virtually overpowered by the uncontrollable crowds, finally gained the upper hand. Their job had been made considerably easier by the impact of the West Indians' fight back for now that whites knew that blacks would retaliate they were less keen to start a fight and Tuesday was described as the first 'relatively quiet' night since the rioting began.[77]

By Wednesday 3rd September the crowds had thinned, and only a few frightened faces were to be seen among the debris of bricks, broken glass and traces of blood that littered west London. Notting Hill was deathly quiet and unnaturally deserted and the police kept a low profile. Pubs, which had been packed during the riot weekend, were now almost empty. Notting Hill had lost its concentration-camp atmosphere: the enclosed, claustrophobic feeling had gone and peace swept through the area like a gust of fresh air. At 9.30 pm heavy thundering rain began to fall which would have dampened any violence, but it fell on deserted streets.[78]

8
Notting Hill to Westminster

Once the worst of the fighting was over, the semblance of order returned to Notting Hill. Black people began to appear in the open once more, without police escorts, although they still travelled in groups. The roads were swept of bricks and glass and the police withdrew. In Nottingham, St Ann's was momentarily turned into a tourist attraction; several bus companies started offering tours to the 'terror spots of Nottingham'.[1] Beneath these superficial signs of recovery, however, lay internal lesions which would take very much longer to heal. One month after the riots the Caribbean Welfare Service continued to receive distressed calls from black people living in Notting Hill who kept their lights out at night for fear of attracting attention. White people were also frightened of walking out alone after dark.[2]

The riots sent shock waves up and down the country. Politicians warned that Britain could be heading towards the sort of 'colour problem' associated with South Africa or the American South, the assumption being that racial strife was somehow 'Un-British'. 'I think the race riots in Nottingham and Notting Hill were a shock to this nation,' said the Conservative MP, Nigel Fisher, during a Commons debate on the subject. 'Suddenly, on a small scale, we were faced with these same ugly, frightening, primitive emotions in Britain which had, hitherto, always been regarded as the very cradle of liberty and tolerance,

the most law-abiding country in the world.'[3] Lord Pakenham
(later the Earl of Longford) told his fellow peers that 'It might
be an exaggeration to say that our survival was at stake, but
it would be no exaggeration whatever to say that our British
traditions and ideals that we most prize and pride ourselves on
in the face of the world would be placed in extreme jeopardy.'[4]
Newspaper reporters were all the more outraged for having
witnessed events. 'I have seen nothing uglier, or nastier, than
this,' wrote a journalist from the *Daily Express*. 'The murdering
mood, the lynch-law madness, was there all right! This was the
frightening thing I have seen in Britain.'[5]

The riots were reported and debated around the world. White
governments and newspapers in southern Africa showed thinly
disguised satisfaction, relishing the opportunity to say 'We told
you so' and to dismiss British criticism of white supremacy
as the self-righteousness of those who had never lived alongside blacks. The *Bulawayo Chronicle*, writing in a Southern
Rhodesia which was about to institutionalise white supremacy,
adopted a chiding tone and reported the Nottingham riots under
the headline '*The Case of the biter bit*'. 'Now that the people of
Britain have to focus on something nearer home, perhaps they
will realise there is more to the colour problem than just colour.
No sensible person will gain any satisfaction from signs that
the colour problem is now erupting in Britain. Nevertheless we
are entitled to hope that the Nottingham incident will serve to
bring home to the people of Britain the problem's complexities.'[6]
In South Africa the leading Afrikaans newspaper in Cape Town,
Die Burger, said that the riots would further among Britain's
public and leaders 'a humble desire for true knowledge'.[7]

The segregated American South also had its say. In
Arkansas, the State Governor, Orval Faubus, was waging a bitter struggle with the Federal Government over the segregation
of schools in Little Rock. Faubus was resisting Washington's
attempts to abolish the southern practice of separate education
for whites and blacks. On 27th August, when the Nottingham
riots were just beginning, he gained unanimous backing from
the Arkansas State legislature to close any school that the
Federal Government tried to integrate. White children were
sent by their parents to barricade their schools against black
children, and later that month Faubus held a referendum in

which nearly 20,000 Arkansas whites voted to keep the schools segregated.[8]

These events had been widely publicised in Britain, for the most part critically. It was very poignant, then, that Faubus himself commented on the riots. 'What about that shindy in Nottingham?' he asked the *Daily Express*. 'We have sympathy for you.'[9]

Statements of sympathy from advocates of apartheid merely heightened the sense of moral panic. Some demonstration was needed to restore confidence in Britain at home and in the eyes of the world – and this was provided by the courts. The nine white youths who had cruised round Notting Hill and Shepherds Bush on 23rd August 'nigger hunting' were given a show-case trial in a packed court-room in the Old Bailey. Under cross-examination only one of the nine youths expressed any regret. The others offered mitigating phrases such as 'Anyway, I hate niggers' or 'I whacked that nigger only a couple of times.'[10] Summing up, Justice Salmon told them: 'It was you men who started the whole of this violence in Notting Hill. You are a minute and insignificant section of the population who have brought shame upon the district in which you lived and have filled the whole nation with horror, indignation and disgust.'[11]

Harsh words, to accompany a tough sentence: four years in prison for each of the nine men. As the sentence was pronounced there was a gasp from every part of the court. A woman struggled to her feet, gesticulating as though she were drowning, and was taken out in tears.[12] Salmon's ruling sent ripples through the white communities of Notting Dale and other parts of London. 'Four years was unheard of then,' says Peter Taylor from the Dale. 'The longest sentence was twelve or eighteen months – and that was for serious robbery. It knocked the pipes right out of our mouths, I can tell you.'[13]

Other firm sentences were meted out to rioters. Five white youths, aged between 17 and 23, all but one of them from Notting Dale, were charged with causing an affray and attacking the police on Sunday 31st August and sentenced to between eighteen months and two years in prison. The Recorder in this case, Sir Gerald Dodson, told them: 'By your conduct you have put the clock back 300 years and disgraced yourselves and your families. As a growing menace, street warfare has made it necessary to sternly enforce the law if society is to be rescued from the miseries of the middle ages.'[14]

The deterrent sentences meted out by Justices Salmon and Dodson played a crucial role in the prevention of further outbreaks of rioting. They made the rioters think twice about risking imprisonment by attacking black people, as one of the Notting Hill rioters showed when he was asked after the Salmon sentence whether it would affect his street activities. He said that he had now stopped carrying a flick knife and had disposed of his gun. 'That Salmon is a Communist. Four years, four years is a long time. Nah, I ain't going to the nick for any nigger.'[15]

A total of around 100 people were arrested during the riots, of whom 73 were white and 34 black. Average sentences ranged from fines of between £1 and £30 to short prison sentences. Running through most of these cases was the legal assumption that what was reprobate about the white rioters' actions was their violent methods, not their racist motives. By divorcing the racial from the violent components of these incidents of racial violence, the courts at times came dangerously close to condoning the former while condemning the latter. One 17-year-old labourer involved in the riots was alleged in court to have said: 'We must get rid of those niggers.' The magistrate, E.R. Guest, discharged him with the following avuncular advice: 'If you have an object at heart like the one you spoke of, you can't try to get it by breaking the law. If you want to get something done, do it by attending public meetings and in other proper ways. Be a man who helps and not a man who hinders.'[16]

The notion that racist views could be expressed in 'proper ways' also influenced the courts' handling of fascist agitators. When Alexander Marshall was brought to court for distributing a Union Movement leaflet during the riots, the police witness described him as the most amenable and courteous arrestee that Notting Hill had seen for a very long time. The magistrate agreed with the defence that the leaflet was 'very reasonable' apart from a few insulting terms such as 'coloured invasion'. 'I don't think it was a very serious matter. It is a test perhaps of what can be put in a pamphlet of this nature. I have no doubt that these political views could have been expressed perfectly properly and it only needs the variation of two or three words to make this whole thing unobjectionable.' Marshall was conditionally discharged for a year and fined ten pounds costs.[17]

Outside the courts a similar tendency to trivialise the riots could be detected within Parliament and the press. Instead of analysing the complex web of factors that led to mass racial violence – the housing crisis, discrimination in employment and public places, fascist agitation and so on – commentators adopted a more two-dimensional explanation. The riots, they said, were the work of those *bêtes noires* of the 1950s – Teddy Boys. Cartoonists portrayed Teddy Boys soiling the British flag with blood.[18] Within this theory, the significance of racism was played down: the Teds were bored of slashing cinema seats so they went looking for a new target for their aggression. One night they happened to come across some blacks and that is how the fighting began.

However, it is not at all clear that the rioters were exclusively, or even primarily, Teddy Boys. One youth interviewed after the riots said 'a couple of them were what you might call Teddy Boys, but the others, they were hard-working lads.'[19] Certainly, the majority of the rioters were teenage. Sixty per cent of those arrested were under twenty, and only 15 per cent over thirty.[20] But they appeared to act with the tacit approval of their parents. 'It was a lot of everything,' says Peter Taylor from Notting Dale. 'The Teddy Boys jumped on the bandwagon, but it was the older generation who started it.'[21] The dubious emphasis on Teddy Boy hooliganism merely served to belittle the wider significance of the riots, and to deflect attention away from the authorities who had allowed racial antagonism and violence to escalate.

The Teddy Boys were not the only group held responsible for the unrest. On 2nd September, at the height of the rioting, the *Daily Mail* carried an article headlined: 'Should we let them keep coming in?' Its author, Labour MP Maurice Edelman (Coventry North), called for immigration control and the deportation of 'anti-social elements'. He was referring, of course, to the West Indians. If they were to continue being attacked, he said, it was in black people's own interest to be kept out of Britain. The Government should restrict entry to only those immigrants who could prove they had a job and accommodation waiting for them.[22]

The next day the *Mail's* front-page leader praised the two Nottingham MPs, Cordeaux and Harrison, for demanding an end to unrestricted immigration. 'This may be the wrong answer, but at least it is an attempt to be helpful. Britain is already an overcrowded island, haunted always by thoughts of unemployment. If immigration is allowed to go on unchecked the evil will not diminish but will grow. Now it must be tackled.'[23]

The tabloid press followed the precedent set by the courts, castigating the violent methods of the rioters but condoning their racist objectives. The *Daily Mirror* claimed to be disgusted by the riots. 'Every decent person in this country is ashamed of the outbreak of race rioting and hooliganism in British streets. It has come like a kick in the pants to all of us. We have lectured other countries, but failed to prevent the stinking explosion in our own back yard.' The paper accepted that it was guilty of assuming that race riots could never happen here, and urged action to prevent them occuring again.

But what action did the newspaper recommend? 'Some of the coloured people who have settled here are no-goods. . . Our law must be amended so that they can be thrown out of Britain. In the West Indies people take far too rosy a view of the Mother Country. They have heard about the milk-and-honey welfare state, with its golden pavements, pensions for all and false teeth on the cheap.' As if the West Indians were rushing over to England for a set of free dentures. The *Mirror's* conclusion was slapped right across the page in large bold print: 'The Government must not dither for fear of being considered unsympathetic to the coloured immigrants.'[24]

The first edition of *The People* after the riots showed a similar inconsistency, denouncing racial prejudice on one page and calling for an end to black immigration on another. It was as if the newspaper were saying to white racists: 'You have no reason to hate black people, but because you do they should be stopped from coming.' One article argued that racism was a disease which could only be cured by convincing xenophobes that their fears were based on pure fantasy.[25] But in the very same edition the leading article, headlined '*Stop them now*', said that the solution to the 'colour problem' was not education but immigration control. 'It is not the shade of their skin that is to blame. It is the simple fact that the immense majority come from backward countries and have a very different way of life from ours. So they tend to worsen slum conditions by overcrowding on a scale that offends their neighbours. The men immigrants outnumber women to an alarming extent. The result – "competition" for white girls that frequently brings out the worst in both white and black.'[26]

This article briefly condemned the white rioters, calling them 'mutual misfits in need of a brain wash'. But its harshest words were reserved for the Government. 'The race riots are the lunatic and criminal result of our failure to tackle the colour problem.' The entry of black people had to be stopped NOW. 'We owe it to ourselves – if we want to appear before the rest of the world as a great people untainted by race prejudice.'[27]

Tabloid coverage of this sort bore remarkable similarities to the diatribes of the fascist organisations. Jeffrey Hamm, editor of the Union Movement's organ, *Action*, said 'The *Daily Mirror* is expressing our policy. Anyone who says restrict immigration and deport undesirables is repeating parrot-like what we said five years ago.'[28]

The call for immigration control was by no means confined to the tabloid press. The *Daily Telegraph* said on 2nd September – while the riots were still raging – that 'even if West Indians or Pakistanis had white skins, it would be necessary to consider whether this small island could absorb a limitless number.'[29] Indeed, the overwhelming message from the press was that the time had come to stop the flow of black people into Britain.

The call for immigration control raised in the wake of the riots was not universally supported. A minority of national newspapers warned against it. *The Times* sympathised with the desire to deport black criminals but towed a pragmatic line, opposing control on the grounds that it would be undiplomatic in terms of Commonwealth relations.[30] The *Observer* adopted a more principled stance, arguing that restricting the entry of black people was equivalent to the route chosen by Australia in her White Australia policy and by South Africa in apartheid. 'For us to adopt it would be a shameful admission that the

problem is too difficult for us to solve and that a multi-racial
society is impossible.'[31]

But if immigration control was not the answer to racial
violence, what was? The most popular suggestion among both
liberal and socialist circles was that racial hatred should be
dissipated through education. Racism was bred through ignorance and it could therefore be eradicated through education
in schools and through government information campaigns.
As the *Manchester Guardian* put it: 'The real cure is a public
opinion thoroughly alive to the virtues of tolerance and the evils
of racial hatred.'[32] Moral education was also the theme pursued
by progressive clerics. Father Trevor Huddleston commented
from his priory in Holland Park that if the riots 'should lead to
restrictive legislation, then it will be evident that this country
positively desires a colour bar and is prepared to enforce one.
But if it should lead, as it still may, to a radical searching of the
conscience on the part of ordinary citizens, then much good will
have come out of evil.'[33]

Although education was one important channel through
which ignorance and prejudice could be challenged, it was
clearly a long-term solution. Those liberal commentators who
believed that education would eradicate Britain's 'colour problem' virtually overnight were being somewhat naïve. But
other, more immediate, plans were also aired. The Labour
Party proposed measures designed to ameliorate the conditions
which had aggravated racial tensions. In a statement released
shortly after the riots, it called for a major initiative to improve
housing in Notting Hill and other run-down inner city areas. It
also proposed legislation to outlaw discrimination in dance halls,
public places and hotels, although the Party still shied away
from banning discrimination in private rented housing, which
it thought unenforceable. The Labour Party went as far as to
consider introducing contract compliance – the system whereby
government contracts are withheld from discriminatory businesses – a policy which had to wait more than twenty years before
the GLC implemented it for the first time in 1982.[34]

These ideas were not particularly sophisticated, nor very
far-reaching. But by removing the worst excesses of the colour
bar and by beginning to inform the public about who black
people were and where they had come from, they could have

laid the foundations of a society committed to equality between races. It was a vision which provided a real alternative to immigration control. Certainly, control was a more immediate and less ephemeral concept, designed for mass consumption, and it therefore appealed to those politicians with their eye on the ballot box. But it was the easy way out, pandering to the racial prejudices of the rioters rather than challenging them. In that sense it was no solution. As *The Times* put it, immigration control was a 'counsel of despair'.[35]

Cyril Osborne, doyen of the parliamentary movement to keep blacks out of Britain, was one of the first politicians to comment on the disturbances. On 27th August, just after the first eruptions in Nottingham, he made a public statement drawing an analogy between the riots and the struggle over segregated schools in Arkansas: 'We are sowing the seeds of another Little Rock and it is tragic. To bring the problem into this country with our eyes open is doing the gravest disservice to our grandchildren, who will curse us for our lack of courage. I regard the Nottingham incident as a red light to us all.'[36] Later he told the House of Commons that unless immigration were stopped, Britain would become so cramped with black people carrying tuberculosis and leprosy, living off the dole and turning whole areas into slums, that there would hardly be standing room. He warned that unless changes were made soon, there would be Notting Hill incidents 'over and over again'.[37]

On 3rd September, while broken glass and bricks still lay strewn over the streets of his constituency, the Notting Hill MP, George Rogers, announced that in his opinion the riots were not the work of Teddy Boy hooligans as some had suggested, but the legitimate reaction of the local community to undesirable sections of the black population.[38] Violence had been provoked by blacks refusing to adapt to the British Way of Life. Rogers produced a three-point plan for ameliorating racial antagonism.[39] First, in order to prevent the build up of ghettoes, black people should be taken out of areas like Notting Hill and scattered across the country. Second, the police should be given increased powers to deal with vice and crime in the area, especially prostitution. Special black constables should be appointed to infiltrate Notting Hill's seething black criminal underworld. 'I don't want coloured men in uniform,' Rogers said, 'but I do want coloured plain clothes detectives who could mix with coloured men themselves.'[40] Finally, Rogers wanted legislation which would allow the deportation of immigrants convicted of crimes of vice or violence and limit the right of entry to those who could show that they had a home to go to.

Donald Chesworth, Notting Hill's representative on the LCC in 1958, remembers being called by Rogers just after the riots. The BBC had arranged for them to be interviewed together, discussing their reactions to the riots – Rogers proposing immigration control and Chesworth supporting educational and legislative attempts to combat discrimination. According to Chesworth, Rogers warned him very directly that if he turned up for the interview Rogers would make sure he was never reselected in Notting Hill. Chesworth attended the interview, undeterred.[41] Rogers' outspoken views and heavy-handed style of diplomacy even commended him to the fascists. Jeffrey Hamm said: 'I welcome Mr Rogers' conversion and look forward to his application for membership. I haven't received it yet.'[42]

Although Rogers' and Osborne's outbursts attracted some media interest, the question on everybody's lips was how would the Government react to the riots? To their surprise and consternation, Harold Macmillan and his Ministers remained silent throughout the disturbances. They made no official pronouncement of any kind, which drew acerbic comments from the press. *The Manchester Guardian* said that 'a plain statement from the Prime Minister would help. Whatever the merits of immigration policy, he can say unequivocally that each of us must uphold the dignity of other citizens in this country, regardless of colour.'[43] The west London magistrate, E.R. Guest, was alarmed by the lack of official guidance. On 2nd September he said in court: 'I had hoped that by now some civic, spiritual, industrial or political leader with great influence in this neighbourhood would have had the opportunity to say something in order to assist the restoration of decent life here.'[44] Visiting dignatories were even more bemused. Donald Granado, Trinidad's Labour Minister, toured Notting Hill the day after the riots. 'Why on earth,' he asked, 'has no single influential person said a word? Where are your Ministers, your Home Secretary? Why aren't these people trying to influence public opinion?'[45]

Behind the scenes, the Government was stalling for time, uncertain about what message it should give the nation. On the one hand, the Cabinet was convinced that immigration control would eventually be necessary. Its draft Immigration Bill had been sitting on a shelf in the Home Office gathering dust for the past three years and the Conservative Government was under increasing pressure from the right of the Party to introduce it.

But pulling the Cabinet in the other direction was diplomatic pressure from the colonies. Colonial governments in Africa and the West Indies were horrified by news of the riots, having always assumed that the Mother Country was above such primitive spectacles. Norman Manley, Jamaica's Chief Minister, said: 'The struggle for racial decency in the West is profoundly affected by these incidents. It is much more tragic than Little Rock for the West. Anything in England which enabled the leaders in Little Rock to boast and smirk is a disaster.'[46] Abubakar Tafawa-Balewa, the Prime Minister of Nigeria, said he would fight tooth and nail any restriction placed on the right of black British citizens to come here. 'We believe that such legislation will, at best, be a progressive form of apartheid and will do irreparable damage to Commonwealth unity, solidarity and mutual understanding.'[47]

Governments in the West Indies were so disturbed by the riots that they sent special delegations to investigate. Trinidad sent its Labour Minister, Donald Granado; the new West Indies Federal Government despatched Dr Carl Lacorbiniere, its Deputy Prime Minister; and Dr Hugh Cummins, Prime Minister of Barbados, flew over in person. Together, they spent several days talking to local residents in Notting Hill and Nottingham. It is a sobering thought that while these politicians travelled five thousand miles from the West Indies to visit the riot areas, no senior British politician made the ten-mile journey from Westminster to Notting Hill.

The visit that captured the public's imagination was that of Norman Manley. As leader of the most powerful country in the British West Indies, Manley commanded considerable political respect and his ten-day tour was given front-page coverage. Manley arrived in London on 5th September, two days after the Notting Hill riots, saying 'I have come to help, not to quarrel'. During his visit he met the Home Secretary, R.A. Butler and the Colonial Secretary, Alan Lennox-Boyd and told them of his stern opposition to immigration control. If England's economic demands required restrictions that was England's problem, he said. It would be a tragic compromise of principle with expediency to let the riots force Britain on an entirely new course. Changing the open door policy would have a profound effect throughout the Commonwealth and would strike a fatal blow in the confidence that the world had in Great Britain.[48] Manley was clearly angered by those politicians who had raised the banner of control at such a sensitive moment. 'The problem of violence is an immediate and urgent one,' he said. 'All talk of restricting immigration at this time should be set aside till the atmosphere has decisively changed.'[49]

Manley's sabre-rattling was enough to check any plans within the Cabinet for immigration legislation and on 3rd September Downing Street finally broke its awkward silence. An official statement on the riots was released which tried desperately to deflect world attention away from the embarrassing events of the past week. 'It is important that the significance of these incidents should not be exaggerated at home or abroad,' said the Government.[50] The statement also touched on the issue of immigration, treading uneasily between Osborne's demand for control and the colonies' equally vociferous rejection of it. As a sop to Osborne and the immigration lobby, the statement read: 'For some little time the Government has been examining the free entry of immigrants from Commonwealth and colonial countries. The Government's study of immigration policy and its implications and effects on employment will continue.' But anticipating objections from Manley and his fellow colonial leaders, the Government added that it had no intention of making any long-term decisions except after careful consideration of the problem as a whole. A few days later R.A. Butler announced that the Government would not be interfering with the open door policy, adding that he had no intention of being dictated to by 'extremist elements'.[51]

Possibly, he was thinking of his own back-benches. The immigration debate within the Tory Party reached its peak a month after the riots at the annual Party Conference in Blackpool. Butler tried to pacify the Party's corporal punishment lobby with the launch of a new penal regime which he promised would 'de-Teddify the Teddy Boys'. A dose of severe discipline – the forerunner of the short-sharp-shock treatment – would instil a 'wholesome dread of punishment' in otherwise impenitent youths. He hoped this would ensure that the terrible difficulty which the country was suffering would be no more than a passing phenomenon.[52]

But this failed to satisfy the immigration control lobby. Norman Pannell MP introduced a motion calling for entry restrictions and the power to deport immigrants convicted of serious criminal offences. The motion was carefully worded in non-discriminatory language, but during the debate Pannell left no doubt about whom the restrictions would be designed to ensnare. 'If, as a result of such non-discriminatory restrictions, more coloured people were to be excluded than whites, that would no more be evidence of colour prejudice than would any general law of the land which coloured people might be more likely to infringe than white people.'[53]

The motion was carried by a large majority. The Home Secretary promised that, in the light of this resolution, the Government would shortly be seeking the power of deportation.[54]

In the following weeks and months the Macmillan Government made no direct attempt to tackle the issues thrown up by the riots. There was no official investigation of the sort that Lord Scarman later conducted into the 1981 Brixton riots. No more money was pumped into Notting Hill to improve its housing and Rachman's racket continued unhindered. The only point at which the Government succeeded in reducing unemployment was during the few months leading up to general elections in 1959; as soon as the Conservatives had been re-elected unemployment was allowed to rise again.[55] Meanwhile the Conservatives continued to oppose legislation to outlaw discrimination.[56]

The first Act directed against racial discrimination was passed under a Labour Government a full seven years after the riots. The 1965 Race Relations Act was limited in scope to colour bars in public places and the incitement of racial hatred; it did not tackle the most serious forms of discrimination in housing and employment. Between 1965 and 1969 just fifteen people

were prosecuted for inciting racial hatred. Five of those were
Black Power activists including, ironically, the founder of the
militant Racial Adjustment Action Society, RAAS – Michael X
(Michael de Freitas).[57]

Legislation to control immigration followed more rapidly, in
1962. The Immigration Act of that year was closely modelled
on the draft Bill which Cabinet Ministers had prepared seven
years previously. The only major difference was that the Bill in
its final form did not require prospective immigrants to prove
that they had a home waiting for them in Britain. It did,
however, introduce the employment voucher system which had
so appealed to Ministers in 1955 because while appearing to be
non-discriminatory on paper, in practice it would only restrict
the entry of black people. To ensure that white people were
not unduly inconvenienced under the Act, the Government
announced at the last stage in the passage of the Bill that
Ireland would be exempt 'due to administrative difficulties'.[58]

What began in 1948 with the *Empire Windrush* ended with
legislation to keep black people out of Britain. This marked the
end of an era. The West Indians who had come to Britain in
search of their 'Mother Country' had now been ceremonially
stripped of their British identity. The Notting Hill rioters had
claimed their prize.

9
Out of the Ashes

'I fervently believed that race riots would never happen in Britain. Never.'[1]

The race riots hit black people like a bomb. The belief that one day they would be fully accepted as British was badly, for some irrevocably, damaged. One West Indian resident in England since 1938 said: 'This is the most disappointing thing that has ever happened to me. I am so hurt that I would like to rewrite the history books.'[2] For many West Indians it was like coming to the end of a blind alley. It forced them to confront face on that which they had always preferred to deny.

As the dust settled and the initial shock receded, despair descended on the black community. 'If I had money I'd tear out of this country fast,' said a Jamaican in Notting Hill. People castigated themselves for thinking that eventually everything would turn out right. 'I blame myself,' said a West Indian woman, 'for believing that they would give us a break.'[3]

The most painful feeling was that of rejection. Physical injuries suffered during the riots would heal, but the emotional wounds were far more profound. 'I don't mind the fights,' said a young Trinidadian woman. 'We have had enough of that back home. It's the hate I can't stand.'[4] Being hated because of the colour of her skin was like being punished for being alive, or having her very existence denied. As one West Indian put it: 'If you ostracise me because of my bad manners, I can mend my ways. If you shun me because of my ignorance, I can learn. But if you slam the door in my face because of the colour of my skin, I am lost.'[5]

The image of Britain as the 'Mother Country' now looked like a cruel joke. 'It just vanished overnight,' says Baron Baker. Right up to the moment the riots erupted he clung to his belief in the 'Mother Country', but that collapsed during the fighting, as did the feeling of living in the centre of the Empire. Afterwards, Baker regarded Britain as a country like any other. The glamour had disappeared and all that remained was the daily drudgery of working to make ends meet. A large number of Baker's siblings had emigrated to the United States, but he had always felt he made the right decision in coming to Britain. Here there was no segregation on the buses or in schools; no lynchings either. But during the riots there seemed little to distinguish the two nations.[6]

Elderly West Indians were the most severely affected. Whereas younger black people tended to be resilient, treating the riots as confirmation of the need for struggle, older West Indians were cut to the quick. They had venerated the image of the 'Mother Country' even more strongly than their children, so they were more shattered when it turned out to be an illusion. Sapped of strength and determination, they were scared to go out of doors, humiliated and defeated.[7]

Three weeks after the riots black people began leaving England by the train-load. Platform Two at Victoria Station was seething with homeward-bound West Indians. Their subdued mood was the antithesis of the effervescent high spirits of the passengers arriving on board the *Empire Windrush* exactly ten years previously. One man said: 'I don't like the idea of children growing up in these conditions – people fighting and crippling each other.' Another said simply: 'England is bad, a bad place.'[8] In a normal year, around 150 West Indians could have been expected to go back to the Caribbean, but in 1959 4,500 returned.[9]

However, it was only a minority who decided to pack their bags and leave. The rest stayed, some because they could not afford the passage home, others because they refused to be intimidated. Baron Baker was one of the latter: 'I was determined to stay to the bitter or sweet end. For me it would have been a terrible blow, having come here to fight in the war, to have the natives kick us out. We were all prepared to challenge it, which we did.'[10] Ivan Weekes was another. He thought that although Notting Hill was one of the roughest parts of London, it also had its joys and benefits to compensate, especially the sense of comradeship and support between black people, and with their white friends.[11]

At the time of the riots, Britain's black communities were fragmented, politically disorganised, and mute. Their needs and aspirations were hardly represented within mainstream political channels. Although, as British citizens, they could vote, many never took up that right because both Parties seemed to them uncaring and irrelevant. Frances Ezzrecco says: 'We got the impression that whoever was in power, we were still suffering. We had no confidence in politicians.'[12] Nor did black people have access to an extra-parliamentary voice. During the 1950s, the black movement was suffering something of a hiatus in Britain. By the beginning of the decade many of the Pan-Africanist leaders, who had been based in London during the 1930s and 1940s, had returned to Africa or the Caribbean to lead the struggle for colonial independence. And the single most influential black organisation in the war years, the League of Coloured Peoples, had disbanded shortly after the death of its founder, Harold Moody, in 1947. Even the West Indians' informal meeting places – cafés, clubs and Shebeens – were troubled by internal divisions and rivalries between people of different Caribbean islands. Many of these rivalries were themselves a hangover from the Empire. For instance, the British used Barbadians to fill the ranks of police forces across the West Indies, which meant that Barbadians were regarded with some suspicion by other islanders.[13]

The riots threw the fragmentation and vulnerability of the West Indian community into graphic relief. Jamaican Chief Minister, Norman Manley, was struck by how unprotected and exposed black people were in Britain. Speaking just after the riots to a crowd of over 1,000 West Indians in London, Manley tried to assuage their battered morale. 'Do not be panicked or frightened by violence,' he told them, 'and exercise every one of your rights without guilt.' But Manley's main message was that they had to develop and strengthen their own defences. 'Build up solidarity between you,' he said.[14]

Manley's advice had immediate effect. When the Notting Hill MP, George Rogers, tried to follow him onto the platform the assembled throng hounded him off the stage. As Rogers stumbled out of the hall he shouted above the din 'Have you no criminals in the West Indies? I will make a bargain with you. You keep your criminals and we will keep ours.'[15]

The riots galvanised the black community into action. Informally, barriers between people from different islands began to be dismantled. 'The riots changed our attitudes,' remembers Frank Critchlow. 'People decided to have their own thing. We used to meet in blues dances at the weekend, socialising, getting to know folks from the different Caribbean islands. People dropped their guards because although we were a hundred people in a dance hall all from different parts of the Caribbean, we were still West Indians in London, we had all suffered the riots, and we had a lot in common to talk about.'[16]

Formally, new associations were established in an attempt to organise and unite the black community. Baron Baker set up the United Africa-Asia League which held open-air meetings every Thursday night outside the Fortress in Blenheim Crescent. The Association for the Advancement of Coloured People was formed by Amy Dashwood Garvey, Marcus Garvey's widow. She ran a hostel and an Afro-centre in Notting Hill.[17]

One of the largest new associations in Notting Hill was the Coloured People's Progressive Association (CPPA), set up by Frances Ezzrecco immediately after the riots with Michael de Freitas as its vice-president. By the end of the year it had over 500 members. The motto of the CPPA was 'United we stand, divided we fall' and its prime objectives were to protect the rights and privileges of its members; to strive for their social, economic and political advancement and to work for inter-racial understanding. Frances Ezzrecco said shortly after the inauguration of the CPPA: 'Our plan is to bind the coloured people together and to make our people speak up for themselves.' She organised delegations to the local police station to protest against harassment, to Kensington Council to demand improvements in housing, and to the TUC to raise the issue of colour bars in employment.[18]

The task of all these organisations was to create something positive out of the destruction of the riots. Politically, their objectives
were neither very militant nor sophisticated. As Frances Ezzrecco
put it: 'What we want is something to be done on both sides. We are
completely non-political.'[19] 'It was more an assertive stance,' says
Ivan Weekes. 'People were determined that they were here to stay
and no amount of fighting would get them out. We were militant
in the sense that we dug in, and claimed our right to be here. And
we made it quite clear that if anyone tried those race riots again
they would have much more bloodshed to reckon with.'[20]

Providing a mouthpiece for the new associations was the
West Indian Gazette, a London based black monthly paper
founded in March 1958 which by the end of the decade had
a circulation of 15,000. Its editor, Trinidadian Claudia Jones,
who had spent some twenty years working with the American
civil rights movement before being labelled a communist and
deported, led the first ever black delegation to the Home
Secretary after the riots. Along with Norman Manley, she
opened a fund to help pay the fines of black people arrested
during the disturbances. Jones had a very firm idea of the
philosophy of the newspaper. It stood, she said, for the unity
of West Indians and all other black people in Britain; and
for friendship with the British people, based on equality and
human dignity. Four months after the riots she organised, as
a gesture of black solidarity and of inter-racial friendship, the
first Caribbean carnival in London, forerunner of the Notting
Hill carnival.[21]

The *Gazette* acted as a forum for debate, allowing West
Indians to express their uncertainties and confusions in the
wake of the riots. Their British identity had been jolted by
the riots, for how could they call themselves British after
being treated like unwanted strangers? This left a vacuum to
be filled. 'Before the riots I was British – I was born under the
Union Jack,' says Baron Baker. 'But the race riots made me
realise who I am and what I am. They turned me into a staunch
Jamaican. To think any other way would not have been kidding
anyone else more than myself.'[22]

Out of the ashes of the 'Mother Country' a new vision was
born. The riots marked the dawn of a new West Indian identity
for black people living in Britain and the beginning of a search

for a common black ancestry which culminated in the 1960s Black Power movement. Initially, the debate focused on trying to define West Indian cultural values. The cultural monopoly in the West Indies of the 'British Way of Life' meant that there was no ready answer to the question: What is a West Indian? 'Because of our unique experience,' wrote Jan Carew in the *West Indian Gazette*, 'we find ourself not knowing who we are or what we are. When a man or a woman says, 'I am a West Indian', he or she knows that this envelope of life with a West Indian address is faceless, a cipher. And the West Indian will only cease to be this when through a creative representation of the smell of his earth and the dreams of his people, he can discover the true image of himself.'[23]

While the debate over West Indian identity proceeded, the new black organisations also had to confront the predicament of how to react to the plethora of committees set up by white well-wishers. Philanthropists flocked to Notting Hill after the riots. According to Michael de Freitas they were 'all of them terribly well-intentioned, quite clueless and full of questions. They wanted to do something for the poor, unfortunate residents of Notting Hill and they were desperate to meet us.'[24] So many conferences, committees, associations, and inter-racial friendship societies were formed in the aftermath of the unrest that one local newspaper asked 'Will Too Many Do-Gooders Pave the Path to Notting *Hell*?'[25]

Some of these philanthropic efforts disguised the lack of any real commitment to the black community. 'It was very *English* behaviour,' says Baron Baker. 'Talk it over, set up talking shops, but when it comes to taking positive action there was nothing.'[26] This was certainly true in the case of Kensington Council. The Mayor, A.N.E. McHaffie, set up a 'Racial Integration Co-ordinating Committee' which held a few thinly-attended meetings and an 'inter-racial' tea-party and then quietly faded. Meanwhile, the Conservative council stubbornly refused to hold an emergency debate on the riots or to discuss the disturbances with Labour councillors.[27]

At best, however, the alliance of committed black and white people had positive repercussions that spread far beyond the boundaries of Notting Hill. Housing became a crucial issue after the riots had exposed the West Indians' poor living conditions and the importance of housing as a factor behind racial tension. The most urgent need was to crush Rachman's empire. Soon after the riots, two men spearheaded the campaign against Rachman – the LCC councillor Donald Chesworth and Frances Ezzrecco's husband, jazz singer Don Ezzrecco. Together they began encouraging Rachman's tenants to take him to rent tribunals. They won to their cause Michael de Freitas, who up till then was still working as Rachman's henchman.

Of course, Rachman was not one to concede without a fight. At one point, Chesworth received thirty letters from as many tenants announcing their decision to withdraw their rent tribunal applications. Mysteriously, all the letters were identically worded and they had all been written on the same typewriter which Chesworth traced to the landlord's office. Nevertheless, Chesworth, Ezzrecco and de Freitas managed to persuade many tenants to follow their applications through and they succeeded in shaking the foundations of Rachman's domain. At the height of the campaign, Rachman called Chesworth at County Hall: 'You're a bright chap, Chesworth,' he said. 'If you drop all these activities I'd be happy to give you £1,000 towards any charity you'd care to name.' When Chesworth demurred he doubled the offer. That failing, Rachman had no hesitation in telling Chesworth he was 'nothing but a socialist demagogue'.[28]

Despite Chesworth's attempts to expose him, Rachman's notoriety only spread beyond Notting Hill after his death in 1962, through his connections with Stephen Ward and Mandy Rice Davies. The Profumo scandal provides one of the most striking ironies of this whole story. For the sequence of events that led to Profumo's inelegant fall from grace, and the eventual downfall of the Macmillan Government, began within Notting Hill's black community. Rachman, Mandy Rice Davies, Christine Keeler and Dr Stephen Ward were all regular visitors to the *Rio*, a West Indian café and meeting place run by Frank Critchlow from 1958. Occasionally, Profumo himself would also spend an evening there.[29]

Shortly before bedding Profumo, Christine Keeler lived with two West Indians from Notting Hill – John Edgecombe and 'Lucky' Gordon. It was Edgecombe who first threw Keeler into the limelight by trying to shoot her in a fit of jealousy outside Stephen Ward's flat.[30] Once this had aroused the curiosity of the press, the details of her liaison with the Minister of War began to be divulged, and 'Lucky' Gordon provided the *coup de grâce* by acquiring a letter written by Profumo to Keeler. So the Macmillan Government, which had been in power in 1958, was toppled partly through the actions of two individual West Indians from Notting Hill.

The riots altered the West Indians' image of British law. There was no consistency to the way in which the courts handled cases accruing from the riots beyond a common desire to stamp out violence. Some judges were sympathetic to the plight of the West Indians. Justice Geoffrey Raphael, awarding a suspended sentence on a black man convicted of smashing a milk bottle over a police car said: 'Some of you coloured men think there is a prejudice against you. Let me tell you this: if you were a white man you would be sent to prison here and now. It is only because you are a coloured man and were subjected to some provocation by a lot of hooligans that I am not dealing with you in that way.'[31] But other judges were less charitable. 'Some of you are what might be called undesirable or misplaced persons,' said one judge, sentencing a West Indian to four months imprisonment. 'I have no power to send you back to your place of origin and I can only hope that the legislature will give us powers to guard against such misplaced persons.'[32]

The fundamental aim of the courts was to create a climate of deterrence against further rioting, and to do this many judges felt that penalties had to be meted out evenly between whites and blacks to prevent either side from taking reprisals. Although the courts must be credited with helping to put an end to the fighting, in some cases this 'colour blind' approach obscured individual mitigating circumstances, leading to fairly iniquitous sentences. In once case two West Indians were imprisoned for six weeks for possessing 'offensive weapons' – milk bottles – even though they claimed they were only defending themselves. In another, two white men and a West Indian stood trial for causing a disturbance in Paddington during the riots. The black man was chased by the whites and just as they were about to catch him he ran up a flight of steps, picked up a bottle, and hurled it back at his assailants. For this, the two whites were sentenced to six and four weeks in prison.

They were joined by the West Indian who was also sentenced to four weeks.[33]

Sentences such as these left black people with the impression that the British legal system was weighted against them. The riots also transformed the attitudes of those whose attitudes had not already changed towards the police. Relations between the police and West Indians began cordially at the start of the 1950s. The popular image in the West Indies of the British bobby was of a decent and polite man in uniform, who would show you the way if you were lost, and generally the police lived up to that reputation in the early decade.[34] Yet already by the beginning of 1958 black people in both London and Nottingham had begun to raise doubts about the ability or inclination of the police to protect them against the mounting threat of racial attack.[35] When the riots struck it was as though their worst fears had been confirmed. 'Black people soon found out during the riots that you can't go up to a policeman and expect to be treated decently.'[36]

During the riots the police were thrown into the middle of a fierce racial conflict. Totally inexperienced and untrained to cope with racial fighting on such a scale, they reacted by trying to impose order on both sides, arresting anyone seen carrying offensive weapons or acting violently, including West Indians. As P.C. Bob Davis puts it: 'The only bias that we had at the time of the riots was against people breaking the law, walking the streets armed with the intention of attacking somebody else, whether he was black or white.'[37] Of course, a policeman confronted by hordes of armed men was unlikely to have time to reflect on the original motivations of a knife wielder. But for the West Indians it looked as though they were being doubly wronged: the police had failed to protect them against racial attacks then, when they tried to defend themselves, they were arrested. Other allegations raised during and immediately after the riots were that black people were harassed by the police who called them offensive names and told them to move on for no apparent reason. Norman Manley was himself asked to move on by a police officer during a tour of Notting Hill. Manley insisted he was doing nothing wrong, but the policeman replied sharply: 'I do not care what you are doing. There are more than three persons here and that is a public meeting. You cannot do

that here.' On the other side of the road was a gang of twenty
white men whom the police appeared to be ignoring. Manley
was livid. He called the policeman's behaviour a 'damned
impertinence', a comment which he later retracted, saying it
was uttered 'in the heat of the moment'.[38]

The riots provided a turning point: not only had black
people lost their faith in the 'Mother Country', but they had
also begun to doubt British justice, law and order. During a
BBC interview Norman Manley spoke for the black community
when he said 'I have a lot of evidence, not that the police
have been unfair, but that they have been unfriendly, and
they have certainly left the coloured populations in London
with a profound feeling that the police are not their friends. I
think it's just as well you know that's how our people feel. This
lack of confidence in the police is something new – it happened
during the riots.'[39]

Although the riots were over by the beginning of the first
week in September 1958, sporadic racial attacks continued all
over London and in other cities. On the night of Thursday 4th
September windows were smashed and a can of burning petrol
thrown into the front room of a house in Paddington. The West
Indian inhabitants were besieged by a jeering crowd and the
house was damaged by fire on three floors.[40] A few days later
Paddington suffered another petrol bomb attack; a pregnant
black woman and her husband were overcome by fumes and
another woman had to be treated for shock.[41]

Trouble spread as far as Bradford. On Saturday 6th September a crowd of 100 white people surrounded an Asian household
and threatened to kill the resident, Mohammad Ibrahim. He
and a small group of friends kept the mob at bay wielding
brooms and sticks until the police arrived.[42] On the same
night in Notting Hill a white man was accosted by a group of
teenagers who accused him of being a 'negro sympathiser'. He
was thrown to the ground, his arms pinned behind his back, and
his face blacked with shoe polish.[43]

Notting Hill remained tense for the next twelve months, and
relations with the police continued to deteriorate. Eight months
after the riots, West Indians were reportedly being beaten up
in police cells or in the streets and the new black organisations

complained that their premises and the homes of activists were being regularly raided.[44]

With feelings running high, Notting Hill continued to be a favourite hunting ground for the fascists. The Union Movement maintained and increased its presence after the riots. In October 1959, just a year after the riots, Oswald Mosley stood for election in the Notting Hill constituency of North Kensington. It came to be known as the 'ugly election', so vitriolic was the level of political debate. Mosley provocatively set up his campaign headquarters in the heart of Notting Hill, opposite a synogogue. For six months in the lead-up to the elections the Union Movement systematically leafletted the area, calling for the repatriation of black people. Their manifesto proposed dividing Africa into two halves, white and black, and on the last weekend before polling day Mosley held outdoor meetings where he told his large following: 'The Tory and Labour Governments have brought this problem upon us. We are going to drive them out of North Kensington and finally off the face of England!'[45]

If Mosley had been elected, it would have been the last straw for the Notting Hill black community. However, when the results were announced Mosley came last, polling 3,000 votes compared with the winning candidate's 15,000. Although 8 per cent of the electorate had backed him – a considerable achievement for an independent candidate – Mosley claimed that the vote had been rigged and demanded, unsuccessfully, that the ugly election be replayed. But there is probably a much more simple and less dramatic explanation for Mosley's defeat. Those for whom race was a salient issue had a choice. The Liberal candidate, Michael Hyndelman, and the Conservative candidate, Bob Bulbrook, could be discounted because neither made overtures to white racists. But the third, and winning, candidate had a reputation for speaking out against 'coloured vice': the Labour representative – George Rogers.[46]

After Mosley's defeat, the Union Movement withdrew from Notting Hill and moved on to other pastures. But the fascists left behind a legacy of hatred and fear that lingered in the minds of Notting Hill's residents. Indeed, the worst damage had been inflicted by the fascists not in the elections themselves, but during the build up of tension immediately before them. Five months before the vote, in May 1959, the fascists' campaign bore its strange and bitter fruit.

On 9th May an article appeared in the *New Statesman* written by Herbert Hill, an executive member of the powerful black American organisation, the National Association for the Advancement of Colored People. Having visited Notting Hill he warned that the riots could happen again. 'I have been assured by the official and private agencies concerned with these matters that the worst is over,' he wrote. 'But I am not so sure. I feel that a critical situation is developing there and that unless some action is taken now there will be more trouble.'[47]

On the night of Saturday 16th May, a 33-year-old Antiguan carpenter, Kelso Cochrane, was walking home from St Mary's Hospital, Paddington, where he had been treated for a broken thumb.[48] It was late and he walked through the quiet streets of Notting Hill alone. As he passed the 'Earl of Warwick', then a favourite drinking place for Mosley's supporters, six white men called out to him from over the road. Cochrane quickened his pace slightly in an effort to reach his home only three streets away, but they blocked his path and a scuffle ensued. With his hand in plaster, he could offer no resistance and he made an easy target. One single stab in the chest was enough. They left him where he fell, bleeding on the pavement.

The murder of Kelso Cochrane shook the black community to its core. Their worst fears had taken shape – racial hostility, aggravated by fascist agitators, had claimed a life. That night, in expectation of further rioting, the police were out in force while West Indians congregated in their clubs knowing that only in numbers was there safety. Frances Ezzrecco said that 'This latest tragic development will open the eyes of those people who have shut them to the critical situation in Notting Hill.' Other black people vented their anger more freely. 'If I'm going to get done I'm going to take someone down with me when I go.'[49] Another West Indian called Danny said: 'I stay in at night, 'cause if I go out maybe some white layabout shout "Jim Crow" and stab me like Cochrane. Then the paper say, "Danny no good really" and many people will think it don't matter that a man die, 'cause he was only another thieving nigger.'[50]

The day after the murder Frances Ezzrecco accompanied a
local reporter to the spot where Cochrane died. It was in the
middle of a residential area, with houses on either side of the
street, but nobody would speak. Two households slammed the
door in her face. One elderly woman was more forthcoming and
told Ezzrecco that she had heard the scuffle and the screams
but had not been able to identify the white men's faces. Then
she went indoors and refused to say more.[51]

A week after the murder the CPPA claimed that black people
in Notting Hill had lost all faith in the security arrangements
in the area.[52] This opinion was seconded by the Committee for
African Organisations who wrote an open letter to the Government saying that, in the light of Cochrane's murder, black
people in Britain and possibly throughout the Commonwealth
had lost confidence in the ability of the law-enforcement agencies
to protect them.[53] The Home Secretary, R.A. Butler, replied
that he was watching the situation in Notting Hill very closely,
but he told senior police officers not to exaggerate the incident
or put Notting Hill in the limelight. This was just another case
of 'relentless hooliganism' by a minority of the population, he
said. Butler used the occasion of Cochrane's death to reiterate
his opposition to anti-discrimination legislation. 'Racial discrimination was not, and must not be, part of our law,' he said.[54]

As for the police, they rejected the contention that the
murder was racially motivated, claiming it was a simple
case of robbery.[55] Despite the fact that there were numerous
eye-witnesses to the murder and that several people gave
evidence to the police, no one has been charged to this day.

More than one thousand people attended Kelso Cochrane's
funeral, the biggest Notting Hill has ever seen. 'You have never
seen the like of that funeral before or since,' says Ivan Weekes.
'It was our awakening.'[56] St Michael's and All Angel's Church
in Ladbroke Grove was full and many people stood outside. In
the front pew sat Cochrane's fiancée, a West Indian nurse called
Olivia Ellington. She said his death, three weeks before their
wedding, had broken her heart.[57]

As the hearse passed from the church to Kensal Green
Cemetery, hundreds of people stared out of upper-storey windows
and open doors, lining the street without speaking. By the
time the coffin had reached the cemetery gates, the cortège

was over a quarter of a mile long. As Cochrane was being laid to rest people stood on tombstones to get a better view and an enterprising photographer climbed a tree. After the service the crowd remained for a long time by the graveside, wrapped in silence.

10
Epilogue

Every year at the end of August, carnival is celebrated on the streets of Notting Hill. Unlike the carnivals that used to take place in the Caribbean under British rule, the Notting Hill festivities have no imperial undertones. No reference is made to Queen Victoria liberating black people from slavery, and instead of Union Jacks stallholders sell posters of Marcus Garvey or Haile Selassie. Today's carnival, which attracts over a million people, is a symbol both of the growing self-confidence of Britain's black community, and of greater inter-racial mixing. It is also a commemoration of the 1958 riots, being held each year on their anniversary, an irony which escapes most carnival-goers.

The streets of the Colville area through which the carnival procession winds its way have changed almost beyond recognition since 1958. The rubbish dumps have been swept away and the brothels closed; the tall Victorian properties have been revamped and repainted and white owner-occupiers have moved into where West Indians used to rent box-rooms from Rachman. In 1958 the streets were covered in broken glass and burnt-out cars. Today they are spotlessly clean and lined with BMWs.

The gentrification of Notting Hill has forced many black people out of the area and only a small proportion of the 1958 generation remain. The leading characters in the story of the riots have gone their separate ways, with strikingly different fortunes. Frances Ezzrecco and Pansy Jeffrey became prominent community workers in Notting Hill. Ivan Weekes became one of the first black magistrates in Britain. Ivo de Souza rose to the level of ambassador within the Jamaican civil service. Michael de Freitas, after his heady days as the Black Power leader Michael X, returned to Trinidad and in 1975 was hanged for murder.[1]

The *Empire Windrush* generation of West Indians are now in their fifties and sixties. Some have died, others have returned to the West Indies; most have stayed, even though when they came in the 1950s many expected to remain only for a few years. But time passes and the harder the West Indians struggle to leave Britain the more difficult it seems to become. The spectre of 1958 still haunts them. For the riots propelled them beyond the promise of the Mother Country into a state of limbo, suspended between Britain, where they live but which they cannot regard as home, and the Caribbean which they yearn for, but from which they are separated by the passage of time and experience.

Baron Baker, now in his sixties, lives in a monolithic council estate just north of Notting Hill. Since 1958 he has put his energies into voluntary community work in the hope of creating something positive out of the destruction of the riots. 'Young people are doing much better than my generation did,' he says. 'We have ploughed the ground for them. We never managed to reap the benefits ourselves, but now our children are.' He is sharply aware of the contrasts between the 1950s and today. Black people no longer walk around Notting Hill in groups for fear of attack. They can work behind shop counters and in restaurants and are no longer hidden from the sight of customers. But Baker also believes that underlying prejudices and discrimination remain. 'We still find it hard to get jobs and England continues to resist the changes that have happened in other parts of the world. They will be late to arrive, but those changes must come.'[2]

Horace Ove, rejected as an interior designer when he first came to Britain in the 1950s, is now an established film maker. He believes that the impact of the riots and of the West Indians' experiences during the 1950s have profoundly influenced the attitudes of the younger generation of black people born in

Britain. 'The fifties generation are bitter and they are sad. You can see that coming out through their children. Young black people can see how their parents were treated and have no intention of allowing that to happen to them.'[3]

After the closure of the *Rio* in the late 1960s, Frank Critchlow opened another West Indian café in the Colville area, the Mangrove, which he still runs today. He has acquired a certain celebrity status as something of a lay expert on the police, having had numerous tussles with them. In 1971 he was at the centre of the famous trial of the Mangrove Nine, occasioned by a demonstration of black people against the police. Critchlow believes that relations with the police have steadily deteriorated since the turning point of the 1958 riots. 'This country has created a monster, a big dark shadow. If my neighbour doesn't like me because of my colour we can still live together. But give that neighbour a blue uniform and he is in a position to use that hatred against me.' But despite it all, Critchlow is an incurable optimist. 'Black and white people are mixing more each day. It's inevitable. Melting pot time is coming.'[4]

Notting Dale has been transformed since the 1950s. The Westway motorway, which runs into central London, has cut a path through the middle of the area. Most of the working-class cottages in the Dale were demolished in slum clearance programmes at the end of the 1960s and replaced with anonymous council houses and housing association flats. Many of the streets where the riots erupted have disappeared altogether. Blechynden Street, where King Dick held his party on the first night of the riots, has vanished and Bramley Road where Majbritt Morrison was attacked now ends abruptly beside a slip-road.

As with former 'Colville' residents, many of the former residents of Notting Dale have left the area, moving to richer pastures in the suburbs. The once vibrant community has been decimated, and while several of the original families continue to live there, they tend to refer to the Dale with nostalgia, as if they were discussing a departed loved-one.

White people are wary of discussing the riots with strangers. This seems to stem more from their deeply-entrenched suspicion and hostility towards outsiders than from any moral sensibility. There is nothing to suggest that they feel ashamed about the riots, and they certainly have not forgotten them. White people still discuss among themselves the Justice Salmon ruling, when nine youths were sentenced to four years in prison. The local mythology seems to have adapted the history book. Newspaper vendor Jim Wright remembers, mistakenly, that four of the men sentenced were white and the remaining five black (whereas they were all, in fact, white). The whites, he thinks, were sent to prison, but the blacks were merely bound over to keep the peace. 'Fair play, the four boys deserved what they got, but don't let the coloureds go scot free.'[5]

Although Jim Wright complains that black people have 'taken over' the All Saint's Road in Colville, where the Mangrove is situated, his attitude towards the West Indians has mellowed considerably since 1958. 'When the riots died down, you could see the friendliness come back,' he says. 'I've known some really good West Indians, some for more than twenty years. You see, I can't criticise everybody, I get on with most of them.'[6]

In Notting Dale white and black people mix to an extent unimaginable in 1958. West Indians attend the local church social functions and drink in hitherto exclusively white pubs and they no longer regard the Dale as a no-go area. Jean Maggs, for one, has lost her fear of black people and counts some among her closest friends.[7]

But she has perhaps been more open-minded than most. Prejudices still abound and racial tension remains a feature of the neighbourhood. John Garrett, for instance, now in his late fifties, is as virulently opposed to black people as he was in 1958 when he joined the crowds of rioters. The only difference is that today he expresses his views in a speciously liberal vein. He says that integration between black and white people is possible, but adds that this will only happen if miscegenation becomes so common that blacks are effectively eradicated. The theory he has heard from a 'very intelligent' friend is that white is the dominant colour, so if there is enough inter-breeding eventually all the peoples of the world will become white. Paradoxically, he then goes on to argue that he would refuse to allow his son to have a relationship with a black woman. Margaret Garrett agrees with her husband. She thinks that it is natural for grandmothers such as herself to want white grandchildren. 'Put it this way. Could you see one of the royal family marrying a coloured person?'[8]

While hatred of mixed sexual relationships is evidently still pervasive, stereotypes of black men have changed somewhat since 1958. Black people used to be accused of pimping, but today they are regarded as 'muggers' and house burglars. 'We imported people to breed the muggers,' says John Garrett. 'We should have learnt from the Americans but we never did.'[9] Police Constable Bob Davis shares the same preconceptions: 'The black people who are always shouting and screaming about how persecuted they are by the police deserve to be persecuted. Not because they're black, but because they're villains. If I want to find myself a mugger in the street I don't look for white ones, because my chances of finding a black one are far greater. They're working in a nine to one ratio, so if I want to catch a mugger, who do I stop – blacks.'[10]

Fear of crime – specifically black crime – grips Notting Dale. Where every door used to be left open, houses now have double locks and burglar alarms. In the 1950s black people used to avoid Notting Dale as an area hostile towards them; today white people are scared to walk in parts of the Colville area where they fear attack from black 'muggers'.

Teddy Boys are back in fashion, early Rock'n'Roll records are being re-released, Colin MacInnes' *Absolute Beginners* has become a cult novel and it has even been made into a film. But there are much more profound points of comparison between 1958 and today. Many of the factors which aggravated racial tensions before the riots – such as housing, employment and mounting racial attacks – are repeating themselves. The housing shortage is as extreme now as it was then and black people continue to be concentrated in the worst housing. Unemployment is far greater than it was in the 1950s, especially among black people who continue to be generally confined to the lowliest, least respected jobs.

Racial attacks are on the increase, directed this time against Asian people, who have become the modern scapegoat. Instead of the argument used in the 1950s that 'black people are taking our jobs and houses', today Asians are accused of 'taking over all the shops in the street and forcing English people out.'[11] They are verbally and physically abused on the streets and in their homes, in the absence of adequate police protection. Between 1984 and 1986 the number of recorded racial attacks against Asian people rose from 7,000 to 20,000, and it is still rising daily and parts of east London have become 'no-go' areas for Asian people in the same way that Notting Dale was for West Indians in the 1950s.[12]

Mass riots by whites against blacks have not recurred since 1958, partly perhaps due to the firm sentences delivered by Justice Salmon and partly through greater inter-racial mixing and understanding. But the threat of similar mass violence still hangs over Britain. 'Make no mistake,' says John Garrett, 'what happened then could very easily happen again.'[13] Whether race riots of the Notting Hill type do recur depends very much on the attitude of young people. John Garrett's son Martin is now eighteen, the age his father was when he took part in the 1958 fighting. In stark contrast to his parents' generation, Martin attended a multi-racial school in Notting Hill and two of his best friends are Jamaican and Greek. Nevertheless, he hates Asians and says he would never marry a non-European woman. In the event of racial confrontation he is clear about where his loyalties lie: 'I'll mix with any race according to the individual, but if there's trouble I know which side my black mates will be on, and which side I'll be on.'[14]

At least today Afro-Caribbean people are confident that they will never again be made targets of race riots in Britain. To this extent, their struggle for recognition within the 'Mother Country' has had some success. This is reflected even within racial stereotypes of black people: in the 1950s they were regarded as dirty, stupid and feeble. Now the image of 'feeble' has been replaced by 'vicious and dangerous' – not to be played with. 'The British will only respect you when they have to,' says Baron Baker quoting Gandhi. 'We weren't prepared then, but we are now – we know it can happen and we're prepared for anything now. If anyone tries anything like those race riots again they'll have a lot more bloodshed to reckon with.'[15]

John Garrett puts the same thing differently. 'If it happened again it wouldn't be the same, would it? We'd be outnumbered now.'[16]

Notes

PRO Public Records Office

Preface
1. Tony Gould, *Inside Outsider – The Life and Times of Colin MacInnes*, Chatto & Windus, London, 1983, 134
2. *Parliamentary Debates*, (Lords), 5th series, Vol. 212, 19 November 1958, Col. 684
3. Dan Jacobson, 'After Notting Hill', in *Encounter*, December 1958, 3–10
4. Author's conversation with Pansy Jeffrey, 13/9/83

Introduction
1. Author's conversation with Baron Baker, 14/1/88
2. Author's conversation with King Dick, 21/3/88
3. Majbritt Morrison, *Jungle West 11*, Tandem Books, London, 1964, 28
4. Peter Fryer, *Staying Power – The History of Black People in Britain*, Pluto Press, London, 1984, 1
5. Ceri Peach, *West Indian Migration to Britain: A Social Geography*, Oxford University Press, 1968, 12
6. For sociological views of the 1950s, see eg. Michael Banton, *The Coloured Quarter*, Jonathan Cape: London, 1955; Anthony Richmond, *The Colour Problem – A Study of Racial Relations*, Penguin Books: Harmondsworth, 1955

Chapter 1   Exodus to the Mother Country
1. *Manchester Guardian*, 23 June 1948, 3; & *Daily Worker*, 23 June 1948, 3
2. Author's conversation with Ivan Weekes, 13/12/83
3. Ibid.
4. Peter Fryer, *Staying Power – The History of Black People in Britain*, Pluto Press, London, 1984, 15
5. Author's conversation with Ivan Weekes, 13/12/83

6. Author's conversation with Pansy Jeffrey, 13/9/83

7. Author's conversation with Ivan Weekes, 13/12/83

8. Author's conversation with Frances Ezzrecco, 13/9/83

9. Author's conversation with Baron Baker, 18/1/88

10. George Spence, 'George's Way', unpublished manuscript, (Courtesy of Ruth Spence), 17

11. Ibid., 18

12. Quoted from Anthony Richmond, *The Colour Problem – A Study of Racial Relations*, Penguin Books: Harmondsworth, 1955, 229

13. Michael Abdul Malik, *From Michael de Freitas to Michael X*, Andre Deutsch: London, 1968, 16

14. The Earl of Listowel et.al., *Challenge to the British Caribbean*, Fabian research series No. 150, 1952, 7

15. Quoted from Peter Fryer, op.cit., 332

16. Author's conversation with George Powe, 29/1/88

17. Author's conversation with Baron Baker, 4/1/88

18. Peter Fryer, op.cit., 330

19. Ibid., 362

20. PRO, LAB/26/55, Colour bars in Manchester and other places. See also: Graham Smith, *When Jim Crow met John Bull – Black American Soldiers in World War II Britain*, I.B. Tauris, London, 1987, 85–6

21. Author's conversation with Ivo de Souza, 27/9/83

22. PRO, LAB/26/56, Welfare arrangements for skilled workers transferred from the West Indies

23. Peter Fryer, op.cit., 362–3

24. Author's conversation with Baron Baker, 4/1/88

25. Earl of Listowel, op.cit., 6; & PRO CO/1006/2 Unemployment in the West Indies

26. PRO, LAB/26/134, Coloured colonials demobilisation

27. Ibid. Note, 27 April 1945

28. *The Times*, 6 April 1988

29. Michael Abdul Malik, op.cit., 31

30. PRO, LAB/26/218 Providing accommodation for West Indians arriving in this Country

31. *Parliamentary Debates*, (Commons), 5th series, Vol. 451, 8 June 1948, Col. 1851

32. *Evening Standard*, 17 June 1948, 1

33. PRO, LAB/26/218, 15 June 1948

34. Ibid.

35. PRO, LAB/26/226 Colonial Office working party on the recruitment of West Indians for United Kingdom industries, 14 October 1948

36. PRO, LAB/26/218 Providing accommodation for West Indian workers

37. Joyce Egginton, *They Seek a Living*, Hutchinson: London, 1957, 65–6

38. *Manchester Guardian*, 23 June 1948, 3

39. *Daily Worker*, 23 June 1948, 3

40. Joyce Egginton, op.cit., 68; & PRO, LAB/26/218

41. PRO, LAB/26/218, op.cit., letter from Hardman to Ministry of Labour, 19 June 1948

Chapter 2 An Expendable Commodity

1. Author's conversation with Horace Ove, 17/1/88
2. Author's conversation with Ivan Weekes, 13/12/83
3. Author's conversation with Pansy Jeffrey, 13/9/83
4. *Parliamentary Debates*, (Lords), 5th series, 19 November 1958, Vol. 212, Col. 646; & *North London Press*, 8 May 1959
5. Ruth Glass and Harold Pollins, *The Newcomers: The West Indians in London*, George Allen & Unwin, London, 1960, 24
6. *Daily Worker*, 23 June 1948, 3
7. S.K.Ruck, ed., *The West Indian Comes to England*, Routledge & Kegan Paul: London, 1960, 16; & E.J.B. Rose et.al., *Colour and Citizenship: A Report on British Race Relations*, Oxford University Press, 1969, 67–8
8. Author's conversation with Horace Ove, 17/1/88
9. Author's conversation with George Powe, 29/1/88
10. Author's conversation with Baron Baker, 18/1/88
11. Sheila Patterson, *Dark Strangers – A Sociological Study of the Absorption of a Recent West Indian Migrant Group in Brixton, South London*, Tavistock Publications, London, 1963, 133
12. *The Times British Colonies Review*, 1st quarter, 1957, 11
13. Michael Banton, *The Coloured Quarter*, Jonathan Cape: London, 1955, 142
14. Ibid., 143
15. Ibid., 145
16. Ibid., 144
17. *Sunday Mercury*, 25 February 1951
18. Michael Banton, op.cit., 142
19. For details of the West Bromwich strike see: Joyce Egginton, *They Seek a Living*, Hutchinson, London, 1957, 93–5; & Ruth Glass and Harold Pollins, op.cit., 78–80
20. Joyce Egginton, op.cit., 95
21. Barry Carman, Unpublished transcripts of interviews made for the BBC on the racial question in several cities, October to December 1958 (Courtesy of the Institute of Race Relations)
22. PRO, CAB/134/1210, Proposals to restrict the right of British subjects to enter and remain in the United Kingdom, Appendix II
23. *Guardian Journal*, (Nottingham), 12 September 1956
24. Ibid.
25. *The Times*, 1 September 1955, 8
26. Ruth Glass and Harold Pollins, op.cit., 80; & Peter Fryer, *Staying Power – The History of Black People in Britain*, Pluto Press: London, 1984, 376
27. Ruth Glass and Harold Pollins, op.cit., 81
28. Author's conversation with Harold Spencer, 28/1/88
29. Joyce Egginton, op.cit., 100
30. *Manchester Guardian*, 5 September 1958, 4
31. Author's conversation with Frances Ezzrecco, 19/12/83
32. Joyce Egginton, op.cit., 100
33. Author's conversation with Frances Ezzrecco, 19/12/83; & Bob Hepple, *Race, Jobs and the Law in Britain*, 2nd edit., Penguin Books: Harmondsworth, 1970, 71; & Peter Fryer, op.cit., 376
34. *The Times*, 5 March 1955, 6

35. PRO, CO/1006/2, The possibility of employing colonial labour in the United Kingdom

36. *Birmingham Post*, 25 September 1954

37. Ruth Glass & Harold Pollins, op.cit., 31

38. Author's conversation with Pansy Jeffrey, 13/9/83

39. Ruth Glass and Harold Pollins, op.cit., 31

40. Author's conversation with Samuel Roberts, 28/1/88

41. PRO, LAB/26/53, Welfare conditions in the factories

42. PRO, LAB/13/42, Proposals by Colonial Office on the surplus manpower of certain colonies for use to assist the manpower situation in the United Kingdom

43. Peter Fryer, op.cit., 372

44. James Wickenden, *Colour in Britain*, Oxford University Press, for Institute of Race Relations, 1958, 3–4; & Sheila Patterson, op.cit., 420

45. PRO, CO/1031/1637, The development of resources in the West Indies as a means of reducing immigration to the United Kingdom, document 12; & PRO, CO/1031/1502, Economic situation in Jamaica

46. The Earl of Listowel, et.al., *Challenge to the British Caribbean*, Fabian Research Series, No. 150, 1952, 6

47. Joyce Egginton, op.cit., 56

48. Earl of Listowel, op.cit., 14; & PRO, CAB/1031/1502, The economic situation in Jamaica

49. PRO, CO/1031/1637, op.cit.

50. The Earl of Listowel, op.cit., 6, 15 & 21

51. PRO, CO/1031/1637, op.cit., January 1955

52. PRO, CO/1031/1637, op.cit.

53. *The Economist*, 9 July 1955

54. R.B.Davison, *West Indian Migrants, Social and Economic Facts of Migration from the West Indies*, Oxford University Press for the Institute of Race Relations, 1962, 64–5; & The Earl of Listowel, op.cit., 15

55. PRO, CO/1006/1, Working party on the employment in the United Kingdom of surplus colonial labour; & PRO, LAB/26/226, Colonial Office working party on the recruitment of West Indians for United Kingdom industries

56. PRO, CO/1006/1, op.cit.

57. PRO, CO/1006/2, The possibility of employing colonial labour in the United Kingdom; & PRO, LAB/13/42, op.cit.

58. PRO, CAB/124/1191, Appendix II, Report of the Labour and National Service department on the employment of coloured people; & PRO, LAB/26/134, Coloured colonials demobilisation

59. Bob Hepple, op.cit., 71

60. PRO, LAB/13/259

61. Bob Hepple, op.cit., 71

62. PRO, LAB/13/42, op.cit.

63. *Parliamentary Debates*, (Commons), 5th series, Vol. 493, 1951, Col. 52

64. Ceri Peach, *West Indian Migration to Britain: A Social Geography*, Oxford University Press, 1968, 2, 22, 92–100

65. Peter Fryer, op.cit., 373

66. R.B. Davison, op.cit., 28–9
67. *Parliamentary Debates*, (Commons), 5th series, Vol. 592, 23 October 1958, written answers *264*
68. *The Times British Colonies Review*, 3rd quarter, 1958, 15
69. James Wickenden, op.cit., 9–10
70. Joyce Egginton, op.cit., 101

Chapter 3   No Coloureds, No Irish, No Dogs
1. Author's conversation with Baron Baker, 4/1/88
2. Ibid., 19/9/83
3. Ruth Glass and Harold Pollins, *The Newcomers: The West Indians in London*, George Allen & Unwin, London, 1960, 58–61
4. Author's conversation with Frances Ezzrecco, 19/12/83
5. Anthony Richmond, *Colour Prejudice in Britain – A Study of West Indian Workers in Liverpool*, Routledge & Kegan Paul: London, 1954, 73
6. Author's conversation with Ivan Weekes, 13/12/83
7. Author's conversation with Chris Lemaitre, 20/9/83
8. A.T. Carey, *Colonial Students – A Study of Colonial Students in London*, Secker & Warburg: London, 1956, 60–62
9. A.G.Bennett, *Because They Know Not*, Phoenix Press, 1954, 22
10. A.T. Carey, op.cit., 68
11. *The Times*, 29 May 1959
12. Learie Constantine, *Colour Bar*, Stanley Paul & Co. Ltd: London, 1954, 168
13. Ruth Glass and Harold Pollins, op.cit., 116
14. *The Star*, 13 May 1957, 7
15. Author's conversation with Baron Baker, 4/1/88
16. Donald Hinds, *Journey to an Illusion: The West Indian in Britain*, Heinemann: London, 1966, 60
17. Author's conversation with George Powe, 29/1/88
18. *The Times*, 28 August 1958, 4
19. *Illustrated Weekly*, 19 July 1958
20. Ibid.
21. See Chapter 2, p.28
22. *Illustrated Weekly,* 19 July 1958
23. Graham Smith, *When Jim Crow met John Bull – Black American Soldiers in World War II Britain*, I.B. Tauris: London, 1987, 85–6
24. League of Coloured Peoples *Newsletter*, September 1944, 93–4
25. Peter Fryer, *Staying Power – The History of Black People in Britain*, Pluto Press, London, 364–7
26. PRO, CAB/134/981 Sub-committee on international organisations working party on discrimination and minorities, 13 February 1957
27. Ibid.
28. Author's conversation with Frances Ezzrecco, 19/12/83
29. Ruth Glass and Harold Pollins, op.cit., 105–6
30. Michael Banton, *The Coloured Quarter*, Jonathan Cape: London, 1955, 134

31. PRO, CAB/124/1191, Appendix II, June 1953
32. *Birmingham Gazette*, 11 August 1949
33. PRO, LAB/26/198 W.Hardman 11 August 1948
34. Ibid.
35. Ibid.
36. *Birmingham Evening Despatch*, 9 August 1949
37. PRO, LAB/26/198, 9 August 1949
38. *Daily Mirror*, 10 August 1949; & *Birmingham Gazette*, 11 August 1949
39. *Birmingham Evening Despatch*, 9 August 1949
40. *Daily Mirror*, 10 August 1949
41. PRO, LAB/26/198, 7 August 1948
42. PRO, LAB/26/198, North Midlands regional controller to Rossetti, 3 April 1948 & 9 August 1948
43. PRO, LAB/26/198
44. PRO, LAB/26/198, June 1954
45. PRO, LAB/26/198, 6 December 1954
46. Bob Hepple, *Race, Jobs and the Law in Britain*, 2nd edit., Penguin Books: Harmondsworth, 1970, 156–7
47. *Parliamentary Debates,* (Commons), 5th series, Mr Braine MP, 24 May 1957, Vol. 570, Col. 1603
48. Ibid., 18 February 1954, Vol. 523, Cols. 2154–5
49. Bob Hepple, op.cit., 157

Chapter 4   From Rachman to Ruin

1. Ruth Glass and Harold Pollins, *The Newcomers: The West Indians in London*, George Allen & Unwin, London, 1960, 48
2. Milner Holland, *Report of the Commission on Housing in Greater London*, HMSO 2605, 1965, 11 & 67
3. Ibid., 60
4. M. Pinto-Duschinsky, 'Bread and Circuses? The Conservatives in Office 1951–64' in V.Bogdanor and R.Skidelsky eds., *The Age of Affluence 1951–64*, London, 1970, 62
5. Milner Holland, op.cit., 10
6. M. Pinto-Duschinsky, op.cit., 62
7. Milner Holland, op.cit., 57
8. Learie Constantine, *Colour Bar*, Stanley Paul & Co. Ltd: London, 1954, 67
9. Author's conversation with Baron Baker, 4/1/88
10. Author's conversation with King Dick, 4/1/88
11. Charles Booth, *Life and Labour of the People in London*, 3rd series: Religious influences, Vol. 3, 'The City of London and the West End', London, 1902, 151–9
12. F.M. Gladstone, *Notting Hill in Bygone Days*, T.Fisher Unwin: London, 1924, 183
13. Author's conversation with Baron Baker 4/1/88
14. Author's conversation with Pansy Jeffrey, 13/9/83

15. *Observer*, 25 June 1967, 13
16. Milner Holland, op.cit., 109–110; & *Daily Mail*, 29 May 1958, 9; & *The Observer*, 25 June 1967, 13. For a lurid description of Notting Hill's resident landlords see Colin MacInnes, *Absolute Beginners*, 2nd Edition, Allison & Busby: London, 1980, 48
17. Ivo de Souza, 'The Arrival in England', in S.K. Ruck, ed., *The West Indian Comes to England*, Routledge & Kegan Paul: London, 1960, 75–7
18. Shirley Green, *Rachman*, Joseph: London, 1979, 86
19. Author's conversation with Donald Chesworth, 20/12/83. For information on Rachman's style of property management see: *The Observer,* 21 July 1963, 5; *The Sunday Times*, 6 July, 7 & 21 July 1963, 5; *The Guardian*, 10 August 1963, 10
20. Derek Humphrey and David Tindall, *False Messiah: The Story of Michael X*, London, 1977, 27
21. Iain Crawford, *The Profumo Affair – A Crisis in Contemporary Society*, White Lodge Books: London, 1963, 127
22. Author's conversation with John Howe, 14/12/83
23. *The Guardian*, 10 August 1963, 10
24. Author's conversation with George Clark, 19/12/83
25. For details of the Act see Milner Holland, op.cit., 248
26. *Kensington News and West London Times,* 9 May 1958, 6
27. Kensington Tenants' Association, 'Report', October 1957, 2 (Courtesy of Kensington Library local studies section)
28. Milner Holland, op.cit., 62
29. Ruth Glass and Harold Pollins, op.cit., 54
30. *Kensington News and West London Times,* 12 September 1958, 2; & 9 May 1958, 6
31. Marilyn Rice Davies, *The Mandy Report*, Confidential Publications: London, 1963; & Shirley Green, op.cit., 155
32. Author's conversation with Baron Baker, 18/1/88
33. Derek Humphrey and David Tindall, op.cit., 29
34. Author's conversation with David Mason, 29/9/83
35. Author's conversation with George Clark, 19/12/83
36. Michael Abdul Malik, *From Michael de Freitas to Michael X*, Andre Deutsch: London, 1968, 93
37. On the area where West Indians were living in Notting Hill see Ruth Glass and Harold Pollins, op.cit., 50; & Colin MacInnes, op.cit., 45–8
38. *Kensington News and West London Times*, 22 August 1958
39. Author's conversation with Pansy Jeffrey, 13/9/83
40. Colin MacInnes, op.cit., 45–7
41. Kensington Metropolitan Borough, Census 1961, Schedule 'A', Section 1 (Courtesy of the Kensington Library local studies section)
42. Author's conversation with Baron Baker, 14/1/88
43. Michael Abdul Malik, op.cit., 71
44. Colin MacInnes, op.cit., 61; Tony Gould, *Inside Outsider – The Life and Times of Colin MacInnes*, Chatto & Windus, London, 1983, 94
45. *The Times British Colonies Review*, 1st quarter, 1958, 18
46. Author's conversation with Baron Baker, 4/1/88

47. Author's conversation with Frank Critchlow, 20/1/88
48. E.J.B. Rose et.al., *Colour and Citizenship: A Report on British Race Relations*, Oxford University Press, 1969, 44
49. Edward Scobie, *Black Britannia: A History of Blacks in Britain*, Chicago, 1972, 223
50. Author's conversation with Baron Baker, 18/1/88
51. Author's conversation with King Dick, 21/3/88
52. Author's conversation with Horace Ove, 17/1/88
53. R.B. Davison, *West Indian Migrants – Social and Economic Facts of Migration from the West Indies*, Oxford University Press for the Institute of Race Relations, 1962, 15–17
54. Author's conversation with Horace Ove, 17/1/88
55. Bob Hepple, *Race, Jobs and the Law in Britain*, 2nd edition, 1970, 41
56. Information on Sarah Churchill is drawn from author's conversations with: Baron Baker, 18/1/88 & 17/3/88; King Dick, 21/3/88; & Frank Critchlow, 24/3/88
57. Baron Wolfenden, Home Office Committee on homosexual offences and prostitution, *Report*, 1957, 116; & Jeffrey Weeks, *Sex, Politics and Society – The Regulation of Sexuality Since 1800*, Longman, 1981, 239–44
58. Author's conversation with George Clark, 19/12/83; & Michael Abdul Malik, op.cit., 70
59. Information on Mandy Rice Davies and Christine Keeler is drawn from author's conversations with: Baron Baker, 18/1/88 & 17/3/88; King Dick, 21/3/88; & Frank Critchlow, 24/3/88; & Iain Crawford, op.cit., pp.8, 35, 108, 109, 134, 156
60. Iain Crawford, op.cit., 127–35; & Marilyn Rice Davies, *The Mandy Report*, Confidential Publications: London, 1963
61. Michael Abdul Malik, op.cit., 79
62. Samuel Selvon, *Lonely Londoners*, Allan Wingate: London, 1956, 77–8
63. Author's conversation with Horace Ove, 17/1/88
64. A.G. Bennett, *Because They Know Not*, Phoenix Press, 1954, 27

Chapter 5　　Keeping Britain White

1. *Parliamentary Debates*, (Commons), 5th series, Vol. 532, 5 November 1954, Cols. 821–32
2. For Osborne's debates on immigration control see *Parliamentary Debates*, (Commons), 5th series:
Vol. 536, 27 January 1955, Col 49
Vol. 538, 16 March 1955, Col 124;
Vol. 544, 21 July 1955, Cols. 537–8;
Vol. 545, 10 November 1955, Cols. 2005–6;
Vol. 551, 19 April 1956, Cols. 1160–61
3. *Parliamentary Debates*, 5th series, Vol. 594, 29 October 1958, Cols. 200–202
4. Paul Foot, *Immigration and Race in British Politics*, Penguin Books: Harmondsworth, 1965, 166
5. Sheila Patterson, *Dark Strangers: A Study of West Indians in London*, London, 1963, 155

6. PRO, CAB/130/61, Cabinet meeting 24 July 1950
7. Ibid., 10 January 1951
8. PRO, CAB/134/1210, Cabinet Committee on coloured immigrants, 4 October 1956
9. PRO, CAB/124/1191, Confidential working party on coloured people seeking employment within the United Kingdom, 1954
10. PRO, CAB/134/1210, op.cit.
11. PRO, CAB/124/1191, December 1953
12. Ibid.
13. Ibid.
14. PRO, CAB/124/1191, Proposals to restrict the right of British subjects from overseas to enter and remain in the United Kingdom, Ministerial discussions, 1954
15. PRO, CAB/1031/1847, British West Indies labour and the McCarran Act
16. Ibid.
17. *New Statesman*, 14 November 1954
18. PRO, CO/1031/1605, Discussions with the Chief Minister of Jamaica, Mr Manley, during his visits to the United Kingdom
19. PRO, CAB/124/1191, op.cit.
20. Ibid.
21. Ibid.
22. Ibid., July 1954 confidential working party of Cabinet Ministers to consider certain proposals to restrict the right of British subjects from overseas to enter and remain in the United Kingdom
23. Ibid., December 1953 confidential Home Office working party on coloured people seeking employment in the United Kingdom
24. Ibid., July 1954 confidential working party
25. Ibid.
26. Ibid.
27. PRO, CAB/124/1191, confidential Home Office working party, December 1953
28. PRO, CAB/134/1210, Cabinet committee on colonial immigrants, 4 October 1956
29. Ibid., 25 April 1956
30. Ibid., March 1956
31. Ibid.
32. Ibid.
33. Ibid.

Chapter 6   The Beginning of Anger

1. Peter Lewis, *The Fifties*, Heinemann, 1978, passim
2. Tony Gould, *Inside Outsider – The Life and Times of Colin MacInnes*, Chatto & Windus, London, 1983, Chapter 8
3. D.V. Donnison, 'The Changing pattern of housing', *Manchester Guardian*, 150 October 1962, 12
4. Author's conversation with P.C. Bob Davis, 21/12/83
5. F.M. Gladstone, *Notting Hill in Bygone Days*, London, 1924, 150

6. Charles Dickens, 'Health by Act of Parliament', *Household Words*, I, 1850, 463

7. Mary Bayly, *Ragged Homes and How to Mend Them*, London, 1859, 26

8. F.M. Gladstone, op.cit., 134

9. Medical officer of health for Kensington, 'Report for 1856', (Courtesy of Kensington Library local studies section), 17

10. 'Fourth annual report of the poor law commissioners', HoC Papers, 1837–8, Vol. 28, 71

11. Medical officer of health for Kensington, op.cit., 5

12. Gareth Stedman Jones, *Outcast London*, Oxford University Press, 1971, 86n

13. F.M. Gladstone, op.cit., 160–1

14. Author's conversation with Jean Maggs, 19/1/88

15. Ibid.

16. Ibid.

17. Ibid.

18. Author's conversation with David Mason, 29/9/83

19. Author's conversation with John Garrett, 20/1/88

20. Ibid.

21. Author's conversation with Mary O'Connor, 23/9/83

22. Michael Banton, 'Beware of strangers', in *The Listener*, 3 April 1958, 565

23. *Manchester Guardian*, 4 September 1958, 1; & Joyce Egginton, *They Seek a Living*, Hutchinson: London, 1957, 70 & 178

24. Author's conversation with David Mason, 29/9/83

25. Author's conversation with Ivan Weekes, 13/12/83

26. Author's conversation with David Mason, 29/9/83

27. Author's conversation with Ivan Weekes, 13/12/83

28. Ivo de Souza, 'The Arrival in England', in S.K. Ruck, ed., *The West Indian Comes to England*, Routledge & Kegan Paul: London, 1960, 78

29. Gallup poll on race relations, May 1961, (Courtesy of the Institute of Race Relations)

30. A.G.Bennett, *Because They Know Not*, Phoenix Press, London, 1954, 54; & Michael Banton, *The Coloured Quarter*, Jonathan Cape: London, 1955, 183–4

31. Author's conversation with Margaret Garrett, 20/1/88

32. Joyce Egginton, op.cit., 26

33. Author's conversation with Baron Baker, 18/1/88

34. Author's conversation with Ivan Weekes, 13/12/83

35. For an excellent account of the origins of racial prejudices see Peter Fryer, *Staying Power – The History of Black People in Britain*, Chapter 7, 'The rise of English racism'

36. Ibid., 142

37. Ibid., 153

38. Ibid., 155

39. Author's conversation with Baron Baker, 18/1/88

40. Enid Blyton, *The Three Golliwogs*, George Newnes: London, 1944, 7, 15 & 16

41. Katharine Tozer, *The Wanderings of Mumfie*, John Murray: London, 1935, 101

42. Author's conversation with Jean Maggs, 19/1/88

43. Kenneth Little, *Negroes in Britain: A Study of Racial Relations in English Society*, Kegan Paul, French & Trubner: London, 1947, 220

44. Michael Banton, op.cit., 187

45. *Evening News*, 30 November 1949

46. See eg. *Daily Sketch*, 19–20 October 1954; *Evening Standard*, 6 October 1954

47. *News Chronicle*, 18 August 1954

48. Author's conversation with Jean Maggs, 19/1/88

49. Author's conversation with P.C. Bob Davis, 21/12/83

50. R.B. Davison, *West Indian Migrants: Social and Economic Facts of Migration from the West Indies*, Oxford University Press for the Institute of Race Relations, 1962, 19

51. *Manchester Guardian*, 6 September 1958, 10

52. Barry Carman, Unpublished transcripts of interviews made for the BBC on the racial question in several cities, October to December 1958, (Courtesy of the Institute of Race Relations)

53. Author's conversation with Peter Taylor, 14/12/83

54. PRO, CAB/124/1191, Confidential Home Office working party on coloured people seeking employment in the United Kingdom

55. Author's conversation with Peter Taylor, 14/12/83

56. R.B. Davison, *Commonwealth Immigrants*, Oxford University Press for Institute of Race Relations, 1964, 25

57. Author's conversation with P.C. Bob Davis, 21/12/83

58. Clancy Sigal, 'Short talk with a fascist beast', *New Statesman*, 4 October 1958, 439

59. Barry Carman, op.cit.

60. Author's conversation with Peter Taylor, 14/12/83

61. *The Observer*, 7 September 1958, 13

62. Gallup poll, 3 & 4 December 1958, quoted in Ruth Glass and Harold Pollins, *The Newcomers: The West Indians in London*, George Allen & Unwin, London, 1960, 247

63. *Glamour*, 20/11/1951

64. *Morning Advertiser*, 8 June 1963, 5

65. *The Times*, 30 September 1958, 6

66. Godfrey Elton, *The Unarmed Invasion: A Survey of Afro-Asian Immigration*, Geoffrey Bles: London, 1965

67. *Parliamentary Debates,* (Lords), 5th series, Vol. 200, 20 November 1956, Cols. 391–400

68. *Manchester Guardian*, 3 September 1958, 12

69. Barry Carman, op.cit.

70. Barry Carman, op.cit.

71. Anthony Richmond, *Colour Prejudice in Britain*, Routledge & Kegan Paul, London, 1954, 78

72. Author's conversation with Jean Maggs, 19/1/88

73. Ibid.

74. Paul Rock and Stanley Cohen, 'The Teddy Boy' in V.Bogdanor and R.Skidelsky, eds., *The Age of Affluence: 1951–64*, London, 1970, 309; for the moral panic surrounding the Teddy Boys see: Stanley Cohen, *Folk Devils and Moral Panics: The Creation of Mods and Rockers*, 2nd ed., Oxford University Press, 1980, intro. & 179–99; Geoffrey Pearson, *Hooligans: A History of Respectable Fears*, Macmillan: London, 1983, 12–25

75. Tosco Fyvel, *The Insecure Offenders: Rebellious Youth in the Welfare State*, Harmondsworth 2nd ed., Penguin, Harmondsworth, 1963, 66

76. Reports of the Commissioner of Police for the Metropolis, HMSO, Cmnd 9236, 1953, 62; Cmnd 800, 1958, 59 & 19–20

77. F.M. Gladstone, *Notting Hill in Bygone Days*, Unwin: London, 1924, 169

78. Tosco Fyvel, op.cit., 13

79. Ibid., 34

80. Author's conversation with David Mason, 29/9/83

81. *Kensington Post*, 23 May 1958, 1

82. Author's conversation with P.C. Bob Davis, 21/12/83

83. *Parliamentary Debates*, (Commons), 5th series, Vol.592, 23 October 1958, written answers 264; & *Daily Herald*, 7 October 1958

84. G.D. Worswick and P.H. Ady, *The British Economy in the 1950s*, Oxford University Press, 1962, 58

85. *Parliamentary Debates*, (Commons), 5th series, Vol.585, 3 April 1958, Col. 1417–9

86. *The People*, 25 May 1958, 7

87. Ibid.

88. For information on the fascist groups involved in Notting Hill in 1958: *The Times*, 10 September 1958, 5; & Ruth Glass and Harold Pollins, op.cit., 173; & Neill Nugent, 'Post–war fascism?' in Kenneth Lunn and Richard C.Thurlow, eds., *British Fascism – Essays on the Radical Right in Inter–war Britain*, Croom Helm, London, 1980, 213; & R. Skidelsky, *Oswald Mosley*, London, 1975, 481–91, 505–592; & George Thayer, *The British Political Fringe: A Profile*, London, 1965, 16–17, 44–5

89. Author's conversation with John Garrett, 20/1/88

90. Ruth Glass and Harold Pollins, op.cit., 177

91. Ibid., 114

92. Author's conversation with John Garrett, 20/1/88

93. Author's conversation with George Clark, 19/12/83

94. *Action*, 16 May 1958, 1

95. PRO, CO/1031/1637

96. *Action*, 8 August 1958, 1

97. James Wickenden, *Colour in Britain*, London, 1958, 23

98. Richard Silburn and Ken Coates, *St Ann's – Poverty, Deprivation and Morale in a Nottingham Community*, Nottingham University, 1967, 11

99. Author's conversations with Samuel Roberts, 28/1/88 & John Wray, 29/1/88

100. Richard Silburn and Ken Coates, op.cit., 12

101. Athelstan Popkess, 'The racial disturbances in Nottingham' in the *Criminal Law Review*, October 1960, 673–7

102. *Guardian Journal*, (Nottingham), 12 September 1958, 2

103. Author's conversation with Samuel Roberts, 28/1/88
104. Paul Foot, *Immigration and Race in British Politics*, Penguin Books: Harmondsworth, 1965, 81–115
105. Peter Fryer, op.cit., 303
106. Ibid., 367
107. Edward Scobie, *Black Britannia: A History of Blacks in Britain*, Chicago, 1972, 207
108. F.M. Gladstone, op.cit., 200
109. Author's conversation with Ron Burnel, 14/12/83
110. Author's conversation with Pansy Jeffrey, 13/9/83
111. Author's conversation with Ivo de Souza, 27/9/83
112. Ibid.
113. *Kensington Post*, 14 February 1958, 1
114. *Manchester Guardian*, 27 August 1958, 6
115. *Kensington News*, 1 August 1958, 1
116. Ibid., 8 August 1958, 1
117. *Kensington News*, 8 August 1958, 1
118. *Kensington Post*, 22 August 1958 & 29 August 1958
119. Quoted from Ron Ramdin, *The Making of the Black Working Class in Britain*, Wildwood House, 1987, 218
120. *Kensington Post*, 15 August 1958, 1
121. Ibid., 29 August 1958, 1

Chapter 7 Riot

1. Author's conversation with George Powe, 29/1/88
2. Author's conversation with Samuel Roberts, 28/1/88
3. *Guardian Journal*, (Nottingham), 25 August 1958, 1
4. Author's conversation with Samuel Roberts, 28/1/88
5. *Manchester Guardian*, 25 August 1958, 1; & Athelstan Popkess, 'The racial disturbances in Nottingham', *Criminal Law Review*, October 1960, 673–7
6. *Manchester Guardian*, 25 August 1958, 1
7. Ibid.
8. *Guardian Journal*, (Nottingham), 25 August 1958, 1
9. *Manchester Guardian*, 25 August 1958, 1
10. *Guardian Journal*, (Nottingham), 25 August 1958, 1
11. Author's conversation with John Wray, 29/1/88
12. Ibid.
13. *Manchester Guardian*, 26 August 1958, 3
14. Dan Jacobson, 'After Notting Hill', *Encounter*, December 1958, 14
15. *Kensington News*, 29 August 1958, 1
16. Tosco Fyvel, *The Insecure Offenders: Rebellious Youth in the Welfare State*, 2nd edit., Penguin Books: Harmondsworth, 1963, 63
17. *Manchester Guardian*, 16 September 1958, 2
18. *Kensington Post*, 29 August 1958, 1 & 5 September 1958, 1
19. For editorial comments on the riots, see *Manchester Guardian*, 28 August 1958, 4; & *The Times*, 4 September 1958, 11
20. *Manchester Guardian*, 27 August 1958, 6

21. Ibid., 1
22. Ibid., 1
23. British Broadcasting Corporation, *Tonight*, 5 September 1958
24. *Manchester Guardian*, 27 August 1958, 1 & 10
25. *Nottingham Evening News*, 25 August 1958, 1
26. *Manchester Guardian*, 27 August 1958, 10
27. Ibid.
28. *The Times*, 1 September 1958, 7
29. *Manchester Guardian*, 1 September 1958, 1
30. Ibid., 1
31. *Manchester Guardian*, 2 September 1958, 2
32. Author's conversations with King Dick, 18/1/88 & 21/3/88
33. Majbritt Morrison, *Jungle West 11*, Tandem Books, 1964, 28–30
34. Author's conversation with King Dick, 21/3/88
35. *Manchester Guardian*, 1 September 1958, 1
36. Author's conversation with Baron Baker, 19/9/83
37. *Daily Mail*, 1 September 1958, 1
38. Ibid.; & *Kensington Post*, 12 September 1958, 1 & Author's conversation with P.C. Bob Davis, 21/12/83
39. *Daily Mirror*, 1 September 1958, 14
40. *Manchester Guardian*, 2 September 1958, 1
41. Ibid.
42. Ibid.
43. Author's conversation with Baron Baker, 19/9/83
44. Author's conversation with Jean Maggs, 19/1/88
45. Author's conversation with Chris Lemaitre, 20/9/83
46. Colin MacInnes, *Absolute Beginners*, 1980 edit., Allison & Busby: London, 178
47. *Guardian Journal* (Nottingham), 28 August 1958, 1
48. *Kensington Post*, 12 September 1958, 1
49. *Kensington News*, 26 September 1958, 5
50. *Manchester Guardian*, 25 September 1958, 5
51. *Kensington News*, 26 September 1958, 5
52. *The Times*, 3 September 1958, 7
53. *Kensington News*, 5 September 1958, 1
54. Author's conversation with Peter Taylor, 14/12/83; *Kensington News*, 5 September 1958, 1
55. *Kensington News*, 5 September 1958, 7
56. Author's conversation with John Garrett, 20/1/88
57. *Daily Mail*, 2 September 1958, 7
58. Author's conversation with Chris Lemaitre, 20/9/83
59. Letter to the author from Donald Chesworth, 10 January 1985
60. *Manchester Guardian*, 3 September 1958, 1
61. Author's conversation with Chris Lemaitre, 20/9/83
62. Author's conversation with King Dick, 21/3/88
63. *Manchester Guardian*, 4 September 1958, 2
64. Author's conversation with Ivan Weekes, 13/12/83
65. Colin MacInnes, op.cit., 190

66. Archibald's article referred to author by Chris Lemaitre, 20/1/83
67. Author's conversation with Baron Baker, 18/1/88
68. Author's conversation with Frances Ezzrecco, 19/12/83
69. Michael Abdul Malik, *From Michael de Freitas to Michael X*, Andre Deutsch: London, 1968, 76–9
70. Author's conversation with King Dick, 21/3/88
71. Author's conversation with Baron Baker, 18/1/88
72. *Daily Mail*, 2 September 1958, 1
73. *Daily Mirror*, 2 September, 20
74. Author's conversation with Ivan Weekes, 13/12/83
75. Author's conversation with Baron Baker, 18/1/88; & *Daily Mail*, 2 September 1958, 7 & *Kensington News*, 12 September 1958, 1
76. *Manchester Guardian*, 3 September 1958, 1
77. Ibid.
78. *Manchester Guardian*, 4 September 1958, 1

Chapter 8 Notting Hill to Westminster

1. *Manchester Guardian*, 16 September 1958, 1
2. James Wickenden, *Colour in Britain*, Oxford University Press, 1958, 42
3. *Parliamentary Debates*, (Commons), 5th series, Vol. 594, 30 October 1958, Cols. 417–8
4. *Parliamentary Debates*, (Lords), 5th series, Vol. 212, 19 November 1958, Col. 633
5. *Daily Express*, 2 September 1958, 6
6. *Bulawayo Chronicle*, 27 August 1958
7. Quoted from *Manchester Guardian*, 28 August 1958, 5
8. *Manchester Guardian*, 19 August 1958, 1 & Madge Dresser, *Black and White on the Buses*, Bristol Broadsides, 1986, 27
9. *Daily Express*, 26 September 1958
10. Dan Jacobson, 'After Notting Hill', in *Encounter*, December 1958, 3–10
11. *The Times*, 16 September 1958, 7
12. Dan Jacobson, op.cit., 3–10
13. Author's conversation with Peter Taylor, 14/12/83
14. *Manchester Guardian*, 20 September 1958, 10
15. Clancy Sigal, 'Short talk with a fascist beast', *New Satesman*, 4 October 1958, 440
16. *Kensington Post*, 12 September 1958, 1
17. *Kensington News*, 26 September 1958, 5
18. *Daily Mail*, 3 September 1958, 7
19. Barry Carman, Unpublished transcript of interviews made for the BBC on the racial question in several cities, October to December, 1958 (Courtesy of the Institute of Race Relations)
20. Ruth Glass and Harold Pollins, *The Newcomers: The West Indians in London*, George Allen & Unwin, London, 1960, 141n
21. Author's conversation with Peter Taylor, 14/12/83

22. *Daily Mail*, 2 September 1958, 4
23. Ibid., 3 September 1958, 1
24. Ibid.
25. *People*, 7 September 1958, 4
26. Ibid., 10
27. Ibid.
28. *Tribune*, 12 September 1958, 7
29. *Daily Telegraph*, 2 September 1958, 8
30. *The Times*, 4 September 1958, 11
31. *Observer*, 31 August 1958, 10
32. *Manchester Guardian*, 28 August 1958, 4
33. *The Times*, 30 August 1958, 7
34. Labour Party statement, *Racial Discrimination*, 26 September 1958, 2–4; *Manchester Guardian*, 4 September 1958, 1
35. *The Times*, 4 September 1958, 11
36. Ibid., 28 August 1958, 4
37. *Parliamentary Debates*, (Commons), 5th series, Vol. 594, 29 October 1958, Cols. 196–7
38. *Manchester Guardian*, 4 September 1958, 1
39. *Kensington News*, 5 September 1958, 1; & *Kensington Post*, 5 September 1958, 1
40. *Daily Mirror*, 2 September 1958
41. Author's conversation with Donald Chesworth, 20/12/83
42. *Tribune*, 12 September 1958, 1
43. *Manchester Guardian*, 3 September 1958, 6
44. *The Times*, 3 September 1958, 7
45. *Manchester Guardian*, 4 September 1958, 1
46. Ibid., 11 September 1958, 12
47. Ibid., 5 September 1958, 4
48. *West Indian Committee circular*, London, September 1958, 248
49. Norman Manley, 'A Challenge to Britain', *New Statesman*, 13 September 1958, 341
50. British Broadcasting Company, *Ten O'clock News*, 3 September 1958
51. *Daily Mirror*, 6 September 1958, 8
52. *Manchester Guardian*, 10 September 1958, 1
53. *The Times*, 2 September 1958, 11
54. Conservative Party, *Report of the 78th annual conference in Blackpool*, 8–11 October 1958, 151
55. G.Worswick and P.Ady (eds.), *The British Economy in the 1950s*, Oxford University Press, 1962, 64–7
56. *Parliamentary Debates*, (Commons), 5th series, Vol. 606, 4 June 1959, Col. 369
57. Peter Fryer, *Staying Power – The History of Black People in Britain*, Pluto Press, 1984, London, 383; & Bob Hepple, *Race, Jobs and the Law in Britain*, 2nd edition, Penguin Books: Harmondsworth, 1970, 149
58. R.B.Davison, *Commonwealth Immigrants*, Oxford University Press for Institute of Race Relations, 1964, 75; & Paul Foot, *Immigration and Race in British Politics*, Penguin Books: Harmondsworth, 1965, 132 passim

Chapter 9 Out of the Ashes

1. Author's conversation with Chris Lemaitre, 20/9/83
2. *Daily Mail*, 3 September 1958, 4
3. Ibid.
4. Ibid.
5. Ibid.
6. Author's conversation with Baron Baker, 18/1/88
7. Author's conversation with George Powe, 29/1/88
8. *Manchester Guardian*, 25 September 1958, 1
9. Sheila Patterson, *Dark Strangers – A Sociological Study of the Absorption of a Recent West Indian Migrant Group in Brixton, South London*, Tavistock Publications: London, 1963, 44
10. Author's conversation with Baron Baker, 18/1/88
11. Author's conversation with Ivan Weekes, 13/12/83
12. Author's conversation with Frances Ezzrecco, 19/12/83
13. Author's conversation with George Powe, 29/1/88
14. *Manchester Guardian*, 8 September 1958, 1
15. Ibid.
16. Author's conversation with Frank Critchlow, 20/1/88
17. *Kensington News*, 30 October 1959, 4; & Ruth Glass and Harold Pollins, *The Newcomers: The West Indians in London*, George Allen & Unwin, London, 1960, 206
18. Ruth Glass and Harold Pollins, op.cit., 207; & *Kensington News*, 19 September 1958, 1; & *Kensington News*, 30 October 1959, 4; & Author's conversation with Frances Ezzrecco, 19/12/83
19. *Kensington News*, 19 September 1958, 1
20. Author's conversation with Ivan Weekes, 13/12/83
21. Ron Ramdin, *The Making of the Black Working Class in Britain*, Wildwood House, 1987, 225
22. Author's conversation with Baron Baker, 18/1/88
23. *West Indian Gazette*, September 1959
24. Michael Abdul Malik, *From Michael de Freitas to Michael X*, Andre Deutsch: London, 1968, 79–80
25. *Kensington News*, 30 October 1959, 4
26. Author's conversation with Baron Baker, 18/1/88
27. *Kensington News*, 10 October 1958, 5
28. Author's conversations with Donald Chesworth, 20/12/83; & Frances Ezzrecco, 19/12/83
29. Author's conversation with Frank Critchlow, 20/1/88; & Iain Crawford, *The Profumo Affair: A Crisis in Contemporary Society*, White Lodge Books, London, 1963, 30
30. Ibid., 1–2
31. Ruth Glass and Harold Pollins, op.cit., 119
32. Ibid., 119; & *Manchester Guardian*, 11 November 1958
33. *Manchester Guardian*, 4 September 1958, 2; & *The Times*, 5 September 1958, 7
34. Author's conversation with Frank Critchlow, 20/1/88
35. Ivo de Souza, 'The Arrival in England', in S.K.Ruck, *The West Indian Comes to England*, Routledge & Kegan Paul: London, 1960, 115

36. Author's conversation with Frank Critchlow, 20/1/88
37. Author's conversation with P.C. Bob Davis, 21/12/83
38. *Manchester Guardian*, 9 September 1958, 1
39. British Broadcasting Corporation, *Press Conference*, 12 September 1958
40. *Daily Mirror*, 5 September 1958, 20
41. *Manchester Guardian*, 8 September 1958, 1
42. *Observer*, 7 September 1958
43. *Kensington Post*, 12 September 1958, 1
44. *New Statesman*, 9 May 1959, 635
45. Author's conversation with Baron Baker, 18/1/88; & Ruth Glass and Harold Pollins, op.cit., 173
46. Ron Ramdin, op.cit., 219; & *Kensington News*, 16 October 1959
47. *New Statesman*, 9 May 1959, 635
48. *Kensington News*, 22 May 1959, 1; & Ruth Glass and Harold Pollins, op.cit., 165
49. *Kensington News*, 22 May 1959, 1
50. *Church Times*, 26 June 1959, 11
51. Author's conversation with Frances Ezzrecco, 19/12/83
52. *Kensington News*, 29 May 1959, 6
53. *Manchester Guardian*, 19 May 1959, 1
54. *Kensington News*, 12 June 1959, 1; & *Parliamentary Debates*, (Commons), 5th series, 4 June 1959, Vol. 606, Col. 369
55. *Manchester Guardian*, 19 May 1959, 1
56. Author's conversation with Ivan Weekes, 13/12/83
57. *Kensington News*, 12 June 1959, 1

Chapter 10   Epilogue

1. Tony Gould, *Inside Outsider – The Life and Times of Colin MacInnes*, Chatto & Windus: London, 1983, 198
2. Author's conversation with Baron Baker, 18/1/88
3. Author's conversation with Horace Ove, 17/1/88
4. Author's conversation with Frank Critchlow, 24/3/88
5. Author's conversation with Jim Wright, 26/9/83
6. Ibid.
7. Author's conversation with Jean Maggs, 19/1/88
8. Author's conversation with John and Margaret Garrett, 20/1/88
9. Ibid.
10. Author's conversation with P.C. Bob Davis, 21/12/83
11. Author's conversation with John and Margaret Garrett, 20/1/88
12. *Searchlight*, September 1986, 5 & 19
13. Author's conversation with John Garrett, 20/1/88
14. Author's conversation with Martin Garrett, 20/1/88
15. Author's conversation with Baron Baker, 18/1/88
16. Author's conversation with John Garrett, 20/1/88

INDEX